Essential
California

by

CAROLE CHESTER

Carole Chester has written 30 travel
books and contributes regularly to
several publications.
She trained in journalism on
Fleet Street, and lived and worked for
several years in the USA.

KU-436-224

AA

Produced by the Publishing Division of
The Automobile Association

Written by Carole Chester
Peace and Quiet Section
by Paul Sterry
Consultant: Frank Dawes

Edited, designed and produced by
the Publishing Division of The
Automobile Association.
Maps © The Automobile
Association 1990.

Distributed in the United Kingdom
by the Publishing Division of The
Automobile Association, Fanum
House, Basingstoke, Hampshire,
RG21 2EA.

The contents of this publication are
believed correct at the time of
printing. Nevertheless, the
publishers cannot accept
responsibility for errors or
omissions, nor for changes in details
given.

ISBN 0 86145 863 X

Published by The Automobile
Association.

Typesetting: Avonset, Midsomer
Norton, Bath.
Colour separation: L C Repro,
Aldermaston.
Printing: Printers S.R.L., Trento,
Italy.

Front cover picture: San Francisco

The Automobile Association would like to
thank the following photographers and
libraries for their assistance in the
compilation of this book.

J ALLAN CASH PHOTOLIBRARY 5 Silicon
Valley, 14/5 Street Car Museum, 20 Grace
Cathedral door, 26 Street vendor, 37
Beverly Hills Hotel, 56 Universal Studios,
58 Windsurfing race, 59 Balboa Park, 60/1
Sea World, 65 Hat Store, 69 Joshua Park,
88 Death Valley.

INTERNATIONAL PHOTOBANK 12 Tram
car, 19 Golden Gate Bridge, 25 Sausalito
Bay, 41 Hollywood.

MARRIOTT HOTELS 73 Desert Springs
Spa.

MARY EVANS PICTURE LIBRARY 8/9
Washing for gold.

NATURE PHOTOGRAPHERS LTD 108
Long-billed curlew (D A Smith), 110
Mojave Desert, 114 White Mountains
(B Burbidge).

SPECTRUM COLOUR LIBRARY 13 Boat
trip, 16 Chinatown, 22 Fairmont Hotel, 33
Balloons, 34 Pier 39, 35 LA skyline, 36
MacArthur Park, 42 Spruce Goose,

50 The Westin Bonaventure, 57 San Diego
skyline, 62 Spanish façade, 66 San Diego
Zoo, 74/5 Napa Valley, 76/7 Vineyard, 79
Lake Sonoma, 80/1 Mission Sonoma, 86
Knott's Berry Farm, 97 Smith River, 105
Sequoia Nat. Park, 106 Yosemite Nat.
Park.

ZEFA PICTURE LIBRARY UK LTD Cover:
San Francisco, 4 Big Pine, 7 Mission San
Diego, 10 Anza-Borrego State Park, 11 San
Francisco at night, 17 City Hall, 27 Union
Square, 31 Alamo Square, 39 Griffith Park,
44 Ahmanson Theater, 46 J Paul Getty
Museum, 54/5 Fredericks, 67 Palm
Springs, 83 Disneyland parade, 90 Lake
Tahoe, 92 Mt Lassen, 94/5 Sacramento,
100/1 San Simeon, 102 Mission Santa
Barbara, 113 Tufa towers.

This book employs a
simple rating system to
help choose which
places to visit:

◆◆◆ do not miss

◆◆ see if you can

◆ worth seeing if
you have time

*Inyo National Forest.
Millions of acres of
breathtaking
Californian
wilderness are
protected in
National Parks or
Forests*

INTRODUCTION

There is something about California that
sparks the imagination! You can't help but
associate it with sunny colours and attitudes,
golden bodies and a laid-back style of life.
We eat the fruit from California – Christmas
dates and out-of-season strawberries – and
we drink the wine – the chardonnays and
chenin blancs. We watch the films made in
California – the old ones when Hollywood
was in its heyday, and the new ones, perhaps
from Universal Studios. We even find
California's flashy fancies and fashions
lovable; it's the ideal setting for Disneyland!
Here Out West, where the lure of gold
brought the original settlers, they do things a
little differently. Here Out West, movie stars
have become mayors – one was even
America's last president. Today's local crazes
are tomorrow's world-wide. Fads – from the
1960s penchant for psychedelia to the health-
conscious 1980s no-smoking regulations – are
taken seriously. But Californians are always
fun to be with.

Whatever you want to find, you *will* find in this narrow state locked between mountains and sea. You will find slick, sophisticated cities like Los Angeles and San Francisco, full of round-the-clock action, yet out along the highways you'll also find smalltown camaraderie and hospitality. You can discover that life blooms in the desert where communities and mega resorts have mushroomed around the green oasis of Palm Springs. You can linger in the vine-clad valleys of the Napa and Russian Rivers, and ride or climb up the Sierra Mountains. California's Great Outdoors is tempting. In addition to its celebrated beaches, the state boasts national forests and parks of outstanding beauty, well equipped for tourists. And the sporty won't have to travel far to find a tennis-court or golf course, hot-air ballooning or good boating waters. Yet this region is not lacking in history – long before the wagon trains rolled, the Spanish had built a chain of Missions between San Diego and Sonoma, many still in existence today. San Diego itself, the birthplace of California, was discovered in the 16th century.

History – and tomorrowland – in one. The state's first capital, for example, San José, today boasts a population of over half a million and, with surrounding Santa Clara Valley, is a world leader in the microchip industry. There is such a concentration of electronic technology firms that the area has been dubbed 'Silicon Valley'. Tomorrowland was also dreamed up by Walt Disney, who

The other California – the hi-tech world of Silicon Valley, around the former state capital of San José

INTRODUCTION

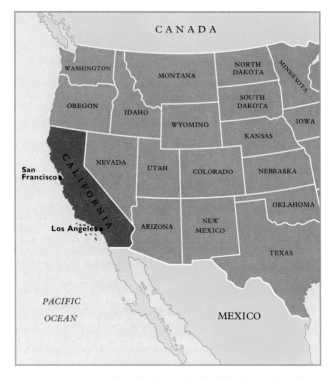

CANADA

WASHINGTON

MONTANA

NORTH
DAKOTA

MINNESOTA

OREGON

IDAHO

SOUTH
DAKOTA

IOWA

WYOMING

San
Francisco

CALIFORNIA

NEVADA

UTAH

COLORADO

KANSAS

NEBRASKA

OKLAHOMA

Los Angeles

ARIZONA

NEW
MEXICO

TEXAS

PACIFIC
OCEAN

MEXICO

chose California for that first innovative theme park. What other country (or state for that matter) hasn't tried to copy the Disney technique, project the Disney magic – without the Disney team, without its success.

Claims to fame are multifold but true for the Golden State – the United States' second highest mountain (Whitney) and lowest, hottest point (Death Valley), and the world's tallest and largest trees (the redwoods and sequoias). It has some of America's longest ski runs and some of the largest man-made lakes; it has some of the country's finest and longest-established hotels and restaurants; it has been home to some of the United States' wealthiest citizens and best-known personalities. How can you afford not to say 'California here I come!'.

BACKGROUND – A PICTURE OF CALIFORNIA

One of the most obvious things about California is its number of Spanish place names. History answers the question 'Why?', for intrepid Spanish explorers were the first white men to set foot on what was, up to the 16th century, Indian territory. Sebastian Vizcaino, one of these explorers, 'discovered' and named San Diego, Catalina Island, Santa Barbara, Monterey and Carmel in the early 1600s. Even the state name was borrowed from a Spanish story and was first used in referring to the Pacific coastline in the early 1530s.

It was the Spanish who sent soldiers and priests to create communities and build Missions, and the cattle they brought with them were eventually to bring this land great wealth. Fruit and vines, too, first grown in Mission gardens, were to boost the economy in future years.

Cattle raising became big business after 1822 when Mexico, having won its independence from Spain and being in power over the area now known as California, issued land grants which allowed an individual to own several ranches. Cowboys came into being, as did the rodeo for the rounding up and branding to distinguish which cattle belonged to whom. The ranch owners became rich, took to wearing lots of silver, and were known as the 'Silver Dons'. Land squabbles and bad natural conditions caused the breakup of the enormous ranches in the 1860s, but their dissolution signalled the start of real estate development.

Oranges and Vines

As for those other crops grown first in Mission gardens, oranges brought the biggest success. By 1872 Los Angeles County boasted 35,000 orange

The first in California's famous chain of Missions was established at San Diego in 1769

BACKGROUND

trees and the idea soon spread to neighbouring counties. Industry expansion resulted in a marketing organisation formed by the growers in the 1890s. Its important successor, California Fruit Growers' Exchange, was started in 1905, using the trade name 'Sunkist'. Today when you tour the vine-clad valleys of the Napa and Russian Rivers, sampling the products which have become world famous, you can thank the Spanish, too. The first grape cuttings were laid in San Diego, and soon other Missions were planting vines – the basis of early Californian vineyards. However, it was later immigrants from other countries who developed vine growing into an industry, most notably the Germans, French and Hungarians. By 1879, about 150,000 acres were being used for grapes, and although Californian wine has only been 'recognised' in Europe relatively recently, wineries were widely fashionable in the mid-1880s.

Railroads and Gold

California, of course, is a land of immigrants, as you will quickly note while travelling around. They came to seek glory and fortune, to work on the railroad, or merely for a new start in life. If there are numerous Chinese Out West, it's because their numbers were swollen by workers coming to help build the railways in the 1860s and 70s. Today's San Francisco tourist attraction, Chinatown, back in those times was full of brothels and opium dens.

The discovery of gold in 1848 not only brought in foreigners, but also a rush of Americans to the Sierra. Suddenly, the state's population quadrupled, small hamlets became boom towns, and new communities mushroomed in mining areas. After the peak year of 1852, many despondent miners returned to other work in the cities, leaving ghost towns behind them. But some adventurers never even reached the mines, like the 'Forty-niners' who were trapped in Death Valley. Funnily enough, California's

Tales of gold drew hordes of hopeful 'forty-niners' to the Sierra. Many went away empty-handed

best-known millionaires didn't strike it rich from gold in that original 'rush', but from a later discovery in the neighbouring state of Nevada known as 'The Comstock Lode'. Men who became wealthy from the rich deposits of gold and silver found there included Adolph Sutro, who became mayor of San Francisco, and James Fair, who created what is now the celebrated Fairmont Hotel. Other men made their fortunes from the railroad and you will find their names perpetuated throughout California. 'The Big Four' – Leland Stanford, Collis Huntington, Mark Hopkins and Charles Crocker – were all ambitious merchants. The first three founded the Central Pacific Railroad and were later joined by Crocker. After the

railroad's completion in 1869, they concentrated on the San Francisco Bay region, the central valley and a coastal route.

The Real and Imaginary West
Not surprisingly, transport was a key to the growth of the West, but its stage-coach beginnings are something tourists still associate with California. Who hasn't heard of the Pony Express and one of its famous riders, 'Buffalo Bill' Cody? Who hasn't heard of Wells Fargo, whose wagons often carried gold and were just as often robbed? Who hasn't heard the words 'Throw down the box' (albeit on screen), originally used by highwayman 'Black Bart'? The 'screen' and films are nowadays naturally associated with Hollywood, but actors and actresses came to California long before Hollywood became a household word. After 1870, the state showed a particular interest in culture and attracted many writers and artists. The village of Hollywood itself first began to be noticed when it played host to the film industry during World War I's temporary stoppage of European film-making. By the 1920s, it was *the* movie centre, where matinée idols dripped diamonds, and epic upon epic was produced. The stars built magnificent homes in Beverly Hills and in Los Angeles' beach resorts like Malibu. And they brought glitter to the then tiny desert oasis of Palm Springs.

BACKGROUND

Anza-Borrego Desert – a landscape largely unchanged since California's beginnings

Film stars, though, are not necessarily responsible for the fads and fancies that seem so evident in California. During the first part of the 20th century, hordes of migrants flocked to southern California in search of work. They came from different social and religious backgrounds and brought new ideas which sometimes resulted in cults that would have proved unacceptable elsewhere.

Natural Wonders

Some of the greatest pleasures for visitors are provided by California's natural wonders, which early conservationists helped preserve. One name which springs immediately to mind is John Muir. He not only gave his name to Muir Woods (a National Monument close to San Francisco), but also campaigned vigorously for the protection of Yosemite Valley. Indeed, it became the state's first park in 1864.

Death Valley, such an obstacle to 19th-century travellers intent on reaching California, is today a National Monument and dramatic sightseeing excursion. Giant redwoods and sequoias, while no longer abundant as in Spanish times, have been preserved in special parks, too, and much of Anza-Borrego Desert State Park remains as wild as it was in the days of the pioneers. Being a coastal state, California's beaches are equally a plus factor. These days, the city of Los Angeles has grown sufficiently to merge with several seaside resorts, referred to as 'The American Riviera'. Malibu, Santa Monica and Newport are favourites. Across the bay from San Francisco, beach-fronted Sausalito has a Mediterranean atmosphere, as does La Jolla in the vicinity of San Diego.

SAN FRANCISCO

San Francisco is, without doubt, a beautiful city. It is built on hills overlooking a bay that is spanned by one of the world's most celebrated bridges – Golden Gate. It is also a sophisticated city which has cultivated the arts ever since the end of the 'pioneer' phase in about 1870 – by the end of the 19th century its opera season was one of America's finest and its symphony orchestra was one of the first to receive regular financial assistance from public funds. But it can also be bawdy – almost as much as during the Gold Rush days when gambling and vice were acceptable as befitted a boom town.

Despite being an important banking, insurance and shipping centre, San Francisco is a fun place to be, noted for its trams, exceptionally fine restaurants, colourful waterfront, and the largest Oriental population outside of the Orient. With less than a million residential population and confined to 47 square miles (122sq km), San Francisco is easy to explore. Its Spanish heritage, charming neighbourhoods and year-round temperate climate (yes, rain and mist, too) add to the magic of the place referred to by John Steinbeck as 'a golden handcuff with the key thrown away'. Another writer, William Saroyan, insisted 'you can't get bored in San Francisco', perhaps because it never went through the provincial town stage. Once gold was discovered in 1848 in the nearby Sierra foothills, what had been the sleepy settlement of Yerba Buena sprang up almost overnight into an eclectic, heterogeneous hotchpotch of a city. It has never been conventional. Most of the streets slant at an angle, and where else would they build an 'earthquake-proof' skyscraper – the Transamerica Building? Only

City lights beckon – nearing San Francisco on the Oakland Bay Bridge

SAN FRANCISCO

San Francisco would put a statue of Ben Franklin (not George) in its Washington Square and suggest that you don't hasten for an ambulance when you hear moans, groans and wails – it's the foghorns. Those who have never been to San Francisco will find the city full of surprises: here a gilded dragon, there a kite flyer or a pavement string quartet. As they say, this is the crossroads to everywhere – served by over 30 steamship lines and more than 50 airlines, and within easy range of the Sierra highspots, Yosemite and Lake Tahoe, the soft-serene Monterey–Carmel Peninsula, giant redwoods and the arty Mendocino coast.

Getting around the city itself is easy, even if not on foot. Riding the metro and buses that operate throughout the MUNI 700-mile (1,100km) system will not break the bank – free transfers are included except on the cable cars. Cabs and car rentals are in ready supply. The ferry service to Sausalito, Tiburon and the islands in the Bay is inexpensive and efficient. It is also easy to use the 71-mile (114km) Bay Area Rapid Transit (BART) system which links San Francisco with the East Bay counties by a 3½-mile (5.6km) underwater tunnel. By car, you can cross the Bay on the city's 'other' bridge, 8½ miles (13.6km) long.

Finding something to do is no problem, as besides the sights and the views and the shops and the Paris-style pavement cafés and the restaurants (all 4,000 of them), there are also the sports and events. This is the home of the San Francisco Giants baseball team, but there is also football, basketball, horse-racing, yachting, fishing and golf. Chinatown's New Year celebration is a festive occasion, and other highlights include a Trolley Festival, film festival, fairs and floral displays.

It is difficult not to fall in love with the place. As Rudyard Kipling so wisely pointed out: 'San Francisco has only one drawback – 'tis hard to leave'.

Cable cars like this have been tackling San Francisco's notorious gradients for more than a century

WHAT TO SEE IN AND AROUND SAN FRANCISCO

A boat trip across the Bay to one of the islands is a 'must'

◆◆
ALCATRAZ
A visit to Alcatraz is almost irresistible because until 1963 it was America's most secure, and therefore most feared, prison, known as 'The Rock'. No lawbreaker imprisoned here ever escaped *and* lived to tell the tale. Its grim past has made it a popular sightseeing attraction, albeit a chilling one. It is thought to have acquired its name from the Spanish word for pelican, *alcatrace*, a bird said to have inhabited the island in Spanish explorer times.

Today you will see the prison exercise yard, empty except for other tourists, with its concrete seats and guard-tower-topped walls. You will be able to take an audio-cassette tour through the main cell block, listening to narrations by former inmates and guards.

Because it is so popular, it is wise to make a reservation for your tour of Alcatraz. The 12-acre island lies 1½ miles (2½km) off the San Francisco shore and is reached by a special ferry boat from Pier 41.

◆
ANGEL ISLAND
This is the largest island in the Bay, taking its name from the Spanish one – Nuestra Senora de los Angeles – given by the commander of the *San Carlos*, the first ship to sail through the Golden Gate. Looking a little like Corsica, it has been used for a variety of purposes, but today is a state park with deer.

Its 12 miles (19km) of roads and hiking trails, picnic area and small museum, make it an agreeable destination for a day out of the city.

◆
BANK OF AMERICA
California, Pine, Montgomery and Kearny Sts.
The focal point of this landmark skyscraper is its formal plaza with an abstract black-granite sculpture designed by Japan's Masayuki Nagare. Locally (and perhaps cynically) the piece is referred to as 'the Banker's Heart'! More important to most tourists is the panoramic restaurant and bar, the Carnelian Room, at the summit of this 52-storey office complex.

◆◆◆
CABLE CAR BARN MUSEUM
Washington and Mason Sts.
Cable cars are very special to San Francisco, although these days they only operate on a couple of routes as a mode of public transport. When their complete disappearance was threatened, private individuals raised millions of dollars, and this, plus money from the state and federal governments, was enough to preserve them. Their control centre (a 1907 red-brick barn sited on the original 1887 foundation of the Ferries and Cliff House Railway Co. building) was rebuilt and reopened in 1964 as a municipal showplace. This Cable Car Barn still contains the operating machinery, but it also houses vintage cable cars, including the very first, launched in 1873,

Loved by locals and tourists alike, cable cars are preserved

plus 57 scale models of types of other cable car, photographs and assorted memorabilia. Forty cable cars are stabled in the barn. During the year they carry some 14 million passengers, a large percentage of them tourists. The cars may only travel at just over 9mph (14kph), but there's no better way to enjoy San Francisco's breathtaking vistas. You do pay to ride, of course, but a visit to the museum is free.

◆◆
CALIFORNIA ACADEMY OF SCIENCES
Golden Gate Park.
A must for anyone with a bent towards the sciences – from fossils to space – since the

water fish are at home. This section also includes dolphin and piranha tanks as well as an alligator swamp. The true star attraction, though, is the Alexander F Morrison Planetarium, where star shows are given several times daily.

◆◆◆
CALIFORNIA PALACE OF THE LEGION OF HONOR
Lincoln Park.
If you have time for only a few museums, this should be one of them. Located on a hilltop, it is a replica of its famous Paris namesake and was given to San Francisco in 1924 by the Spreckels family. As one might expect, it houses an all-French collection of art, including many Rodin bronzes. Entrance is free on the first Wednesday of each month.

displays in many fascinating halls can be viewed under the one roof. It is the West's oldest science institution – moved to its present location after the big fire of 1906. Recommended for children, entrance to the Academy is free on the first Wednesday of every month. American mammals in natural settings can be found in the Hall of Mammals; similarly, a huge collection of birds are housed in their own hall and geological exhibits are displayed in the Hall of Minerals. In another wing is the Simson African Hall, containing hunting trophies presented to the museum by Leslie Simson, a mining engineer who loved the sport. Don't miss the Wattis Hall of Man, nor the outstanding Steinhart Aquarium where thousands of fresh and salt-

◆◆◆
CHINATOWN
Grant Ave.
Almost a city within a city, San Francisco's Chinatown is the largest settlement of its kind outside Asia. The main artery of this 24-block exotic labyrinth of shops, restaurants and landmarks, is Grant Avenue. Where it intersects Bush Street stands the ornamental, green-tiled gateway that marks the frontier of the Oriental stronghold. The quarter officially ends at Broadway. Chinatown is as congested as any Hong Kong side-street, and the best way to explore it is on foot. As befits any Oriental quarter, there are dragon-entwined lamp-posts and pagoda-topped telephone boxes, not to mention the

SAN FRANCISCO

calligraphy street signs. Many buildings have arched eaves, carved cornices and filigreed balconies. Grocery shops overflow with herbs and Chinese delicacies; gift shops are crammed with rare and not so rare art objects and souvenirs; eating places include tea houses that specialise in *dim sum* and some of the best restaurants in town.

The lure of the gold mines and work on the railroad brought numerous Chinese immigrants to San Francisco. By the end of 1850 there were over 4,000 here, but by 1875 there were over 45,000. The community today is estimated to be as large as 160,000. To find out more about the contributions made by the early Chinese to Californian industries, visit the **Chinese Historical Society** (free) on Adler Place. The **Chinese Culture Center** on Kearny Street (also free) features changing exhibitions of Chinese arts and crafts. If there is one tranquil spot in this bustling and colourful district, it is **St Mary's Square**, dominated by the 12ft (3.6m) statue of Dr Sun Yat-sen, founder of the Chinese Republic. Diagonally across from the Square, on the Grant-California corner, is a most un-Chinese edifice – **Old St Mary's Church**. This,

The bright lights of Chinatown, an integral part of city nightlife

California's first cathedral, was largely built by Chinese labourers in 1854 from brick brought around Cape Horn and granite cut in China. Three other more-Oriental religious institutions of note are the **Kong Chow Temple** at Clay and Stockton Streets, the **Tien Hou Temple** on Waverly Place, and **Buddha's Universal Church** on Washington Street.

What looks like a three-tiered 'temple' on Washington Street (and is actually the Bank of Canton) used to house the Chinatown Telephone Exchange. Before 1949 when the dial system took over, the operators here were so proficient in dialects and had such fantastic memories, that they were able to connect hundreds of subscribers who asked for their party by name, not number.

Chinatown is at its most magnificent during festival times: the spring Festival of the Tombs, the summer Dragon Boat Celebration, the autumn Moon Festival, and most especially Chinese New Year.

◆
CIVIC CENTER
Golden Gate Ave.
Said by many architects to be the finest civic centre in the United States, this one is graced by a City Hall that boasts a higher dome than Washington's. In addition to the State and Federal Office Buildings, there is a Civic Auditorium which can seat as many as 7,000 people attending one of its sporting or

Dignified and stately – the City Hall

cultural events.
Complementing this is the Performing Arts Center and, beneath the Plaza, the Brooks Exhibit Hall. Inside the main city public library is an interesting History Room containing old documents, special displays and household items salvaged from the 1906 earthquake and fire.

◆
COIT TOWER
Lombard St and Telegraph Blvd.
This rather improbable structure on top of Telegraph Hill was built in 1934 at the bequest of Lillie Hitchcock Coit, daughter of a well-known surgeon. Murals depicting Californian life in the 1930s decorate the Tower's gallery, but the real reason for a visit

here is the view. From the 210ft-high (64m) observation platform the panorama of Bay and city spreads before you. Even from the base of the tower the view is splendid. The hill on which the tower stands was christened 'Telegraph' in earlier days when a semaphore was used to signal the approach of ships through the Golden Gate.

◆◆
EMBARCADERO CENTER
Clay St.
A highly visible bayside complex, the Embarcadero Center comprises five buildings that house shops, restaurants, offices and the cleverly designed Hyatt Regency Hotel. Pedestrian bridges link this complex to the Golden Gateway Center.

◆
FERRY BUILDING
Market St.
Still very much a San Francisco landmark, the Ferry Building was patterned after the Giralda Tower in Seville. It is headquarters for the Port of San Francisco and the World Trade Center. Before the Bay bridges were built, 50 million ferry-boat commuters a year passed through this bayside entry point. Today, at the terminal's southern end, ferries depart for Sausalito and Larkspur; at the northern end, for Tiburon.

◆◆◆
FISHERMAN'S WHARF
Taylor St.
The most popular (and touristy) district in town! Many people

come to this area to eat in the seafood restaurants clustered along the front, facing the brightly painted fishing boats, or by purchasing fresh fish and sourdough bread from the food stalls and bakeries. Queues are especially long when crab is in season (mid-November to June).

Tourists also come to the Wharf to shop, if not from the roadside crafts stalls, most certainly at The Cannery and Ghirardelli Square, both smart complexes converted from factories. They also come to enjoy the street entertainment – there's always something happening in this part of town. In the vicinity, the **National Maritime Museum** has a strong appeal to children. Located at the foot of Beach and Polk Streets, it contains many nautical artefacts from Gold Rush days. The flotilla of historic ships at Hyde Street Pier is also part of the museum. Here, the last ship of the Cape Horn fleet is moored – the steel-hulled, square-rigged *Balclutha*, built in Scotland in 1886.

Other treasures include a steam schooner, a double-ended commuter ferry, and river and ocean-going tugs. You may also view the last of World War II's 'Liberty' ships at Pier 3 and board a fleet submarine at Pier 45.

◆◆◆
GOLDEN GATE BRIDGE
This is one of the world's most famous bridges, although it's not actually golden coloured! Opened in 1937 at a cost of

$35 million, it was designed by Joseph Strauss and was, until 1964, the longest, single-span suspension bridge. It remains one of the most beautiful. The best vantage point for photographers is Vista Point on the northern approach. The bridge is just north of the city, on CA1.

Never golden, but handsome – the Golden Gate Bridge

◆◆◆
GOLDEN GATE PARK
Lincoln Way.
The place for a little solace, a little recreation, a little band music. Before Scottish landscape gardener John McLaren arrived on the San

Francisco scene, what is now such a popular park was nothing but sand dunes. McLaren discovered that there were varieties of shrubs and grass which would hold the sand in place and, thanks to his careful cultivation, today there is a wealth of flowery dells, arboreta and botanical gardens. A statue of the man stands in the dell named for him, where 300 varieties of rhododendrons blossom.

Another floral attraction is the Conservatory of Flowers, modelled after Kew Gardens, where a large and varied collection of tropical flowers is grown. Six thousand plant species, including rare Californian redwoods, give the Strybing Arboretum and Botanical Gardens their reputation, whilst Shakespeare's Garden of Flowers contains all those ever mentioned in the Bard's plays. The Japanese Tea Garden is a 5-acre legacy from the 1894 Midwinter International Exposition. With its shinto shrines, wishing bridge and miniature trees, it looks at its most authentic in spring when the cherry trees bloom.

Plants alone don't make a park and Golden Gate is also meant to be played in. It has its baseball pitch and polo field, a children's playground and Spreckels Lake for model boats. On Stowe Lake, the largest of the artificial lakes, rented canoes, rowingboats and motor boats may be taken out. In the open-air auditorium of the Music Concourse,

Sunday concerts are given in good weather in the shelter of plane trees.

Within the park are several museums. The most important are the California Academy of Sciences and the M H de Young Memorial Museum (see own entries), but there is also the Asian Art Museum which contains Avery Brundage's vast collection of Oriental art treasures, including some noteworthy jades.

◆

GRACE CATHEDRAL
California and Taylor Sts.
Charles Crocker (one of the 'Big Four') once had a mansion on this site. Today, Grace is the country's third largest Episcopal cathedral, and one of the most impressive examples of gothic architecture in the US. Built in 1910, its east entrance is embellished by replicas of the

Grace Cathedral – a detail on the ornate main door

Ghiberti doors of the Florence Baptistry.

◆
HAIGHT-ASHBURY
Buena Vista Park.
This area of town was at its most notorious during the 1960s, when it was a hippie haven. It has since been gentrified, though nowadays there are punks among the yuppies.

◆
JACKSON SQUARE
A renovated and revitalised area whose history goes back to San Francisco's boozy, brawling Gold Rush days. Don't look for a proper square, however, as it is more of a narrow rectangle formed by Jackson, Montgomery, Gold and Sansome Streets – a redeveloped district that these days takes in some of the surrounding streets besides. The city's first bridge was built over a backwater in 1844, on the Jackson–Montgomery corner, making a shortcut to the bayfront. Then there were only a few settlers – 5 years later there were thousands. The area became the city's commercial hub with sturdy buildings that withstood the 1906 earthquake and fire. But the rest of San Francisco had to rebuild, and the Jackson district fell into disrepair. The neighbourhood's renaissance began in 1951 and in 1972 it was proclaimed a 'historic district' with 17 landmark buildings.
Of special interest are: No 400 Jackson, partly dating from 1859; 415–431 Jackson, built in 1853 and used by Domingo Ghiradelli for his original chocolate factory; 441 Jackson, built in 1861 on the hulls of two abandoned ships; 458–460 Jackson, first occupied in 1854; 470 Jackson, housing consulates in the 1850s and 60s; and 452 Jackson, built in 1850 using ship masts as interior support columns.

◆
JAPAN TOWN
Some 13,000 Japanese Americans are estimated to live in San Francisco. They started moving into the district known as the Western Addition in the early 1900s, and it was not long before the area acquired the look of a mini Ginza, with import shops and Japanese restaurants. The focal point for visitors is the Japan Center, a 5-acre site occupied by tempura and sushi bars, tea houses and craft stores, and the Miyako hotel where you'll find both Japanese and Western-style accommodations. Part of the complex is the Peace Plaza whose main feature is a five-tier pagoda designed by the famous Japanese architect, Yoshiro Taniguchi.

◆◆◆
LOMBARD STREET
Drive down it for a dazzling view and dizzying experience – Lombard Street, often called 'the world's crookedest', descends Russian Hill in nine hairpin bends on the block between Leavenworth and Hyde. The hill itself derives its name from Russian sailors buried here.

SAN FRANCISCO

◆◆◆
MISSION DOLORES
16th and Dolores Sts.

This is the more familiar name for the Mission of San Francisco de Asis, founded by Father Junipero Serra in 1776, but later constructed in its present adobe style. It took the 'Dolores' name from the nearby lake called by the Spaniards 'Laguna de Nuestra Senora de los Dolores'. It was the sixth of 21 Missions established by the Franciscans and its crypts and adjacent graveyard are full of early city history. The Mission is most often reached via the clearly marked 49 Mile Scenic Drive.

◆◆◆
NOB HILL

As its name suggests, this is a place for the well-heeled, including tourists who opt to stay at the Fairmont or Mark Hopkins hotels. The name is a contraction of the Hindu word *nabob*, referring to a person who has acquired great wealth – San Francisco's nobs made their fortunes from gold, silver and the railroad in the mid-1800s. In the years following the discovery of gold, this hill, 376ft (115m) above the waterfront, proved an élitist escape hatch from the rowdiness below. Robert Louis Stevenson described it in 1882 as 'the hill of palaces'.

It remains a steep hill, but happily the cable car route installed by the millionaire hillside home owners still operates. Unfortunately, the grand wooden villas did not survive the 1906 fire, although the only brick (brownstone) residence built by silver king James Flood, and now the private Pacific Union Club, did.

A retreat for the élite, the Fairmont Hotel stands high above the city on Nob Hill

◆◆
NORTH BEACH
Columbus Ave to Broadway.
This colourful neighbourhood
is set in a narrow valley
between Telegraph and
Russian Hills. It was so named
because in the 1860s there was
a beach here, though later the
land was filled in.

Until quite recently it was very
much an Italian quarter. It's not
so solidly Mediterranean now,
although there are still the
espresso bars and other Italian
influences. More than that, it's
the entertainment belt – jazz,
cabaret, strip-tease – with
offerings from low grade to
high quality.

◆◆
OLD MINT
5th and Mission Sts.
Architecturally speaking, this
building is said to be one of the
best examples of Federal
classical in the West – but it is
the pyramid of gold bars in the
circular vault that is the
dramatic display. The museum
also contains Western art and
pioneer gold coins.

◆
PACIFIC HEIGHTS
One of the smartest areas of
the city, shared by consulates
and condominiums and great
mansions fronting on parterred
gardens. The best place to
house browse is along the
Broadway bluff between
Webster and Lyon Streets,
where the Hamlin School and
Convent of the Sacred Heart
are of architectural interest.
Mansions of note include the
Spreckels (2080 Washington
Street), the Whittier (2090
Jackson Street) and the Bourn
(2550 Webster Street).

◆◆
PALACE OF FINE ARTS
3601 Lyon St.
Beautifully restored, this
'palace' was built for the 1915
Panama–Pacific Exposition.
Today it contains the
Exploratorium, a much-
acclaimed hands-on science
museum where some 600
exhibits may be pushed,
pulled, manipulated, etc as a
way of heightening awareness.
Entrance is free on the first
Wednesday of every month
and every Wednesday
evening.

◆
PORTSMOUTH SQUARE
Portsmouth Square is a small
historic park in Chinatown
where the American flag was
raised in 1846 by Captain John
Montgomery who claimed
California for the United States.
By the time New York
Mormon, Sam Brannan,
arrived with a colonising force
3 weeks later, California had
already been annexed by the
United States.

◆◆
PRESIDIO
Presidios were the military
attachment to Missions. This
one, established in 1776,
covers a large area just south
of the Golden Gate Bridge.
Today it is used as army
headquarters. The main
historic site is the Presidio
Army Museum, San
Francisco's oldest adobe
building. The Presidio is also
the start of an ecology trail.

◆
ST MARY'S CATHEDRAL
Geary and Gough Sts on Cathedral Hill.
This eminent church was completed in 1970 on the same site as the earlier church of the Catholic Archdiocese of San Francisco. Rising to 190ft (58m), it is a bold piece of architecture, an amalgam of many talents. Open on four sides to permit panoramic city views, this modern cathedral features marble, stained glass, a magnificent baldachin suspended above the sanctuary, and a Ruffatti organ said to be among the world's best.

◆◆
SAN FRANCISCO MUSEUM OF MODERN ART
McAllister St at Van Ness Ave.
This, the city's major art museum, located at the Civic Center in the Veteran's Building, features a permanent collection of 20th-century art displayed on a rotating basis. Among the famous contemporary artworks on view here are those by Picasso, Klee and Pollock.

◆◆
SAN FRANCISCO ZOO
Sloat Blvd.
One of the top zoos in America, this is a real attraction for children. Among the more unusual residents are snow leopards, pygmy hippos and a white tiger. A popular section is Gorilla World, a $2 million playground for those most man-like of animals, which provides eight viewing areas. A more recent addition is

Koala Crossing, a habitat for koalas, modelled on the Queensland Outback in a grove of eucalyptus trees. Another particularly innovative exhibit is the $7 million Primate Discovery Center where 16 endangered species interact in 'natural' settings. Two-legged and four-legged kids get together in the Children's Zoo section.

◆◆◆
SAUSALITO
The temptation to cross San Francisco Bay to the seaside community of Sausalito is rarely resistible. Sausalito may very easily be reached by bridge or ferry and its laid-back, Riviera atmosphere is inevitably enjoyed by all who wander this way (the view back to San Francisco is worth the trip alone).
Sausalito is certainly picturesque: its houses, restaurants and guest houses are bright with flowers and cling to the hillside in precipitous fashion. It is cheerful, chic and fashionable – California's answer to Capri with al fresco terraces above, bars, discotheques and boutiques below. Absolutely recommended for a day away from the city, or just for lunch.

◆◆
SEAL ROCKS
Point Lobos Ave.
At the foot of Point Lobos Avenue, look offshore to these rocks. Binoculars will bring the shore birds and frolicking sea-lions into closer view.
Whatever the time of year, wildlife can be seen – and you

can even watch the animals in comfort from Cliff House restaurant. The original Cliff House was the home of Adolph Sutro (who broke the silver kings' monopoly) – he created an elaborate resort in this Sutro Heights area in the 1890s.

◆
SOMA
A 2-square-mile (5 sq km) grid of wide, one-way streets and narrow alleys has been dubbed 'South of Market' (SoMa) and is San Francisco's answer to New York's SoHo. Immigrants and the avant-garde live here; warehouses and workshops

That Riviera touch – a view across the Bay from the chic waterside village of Sausalito

have become dance clubs and restaurants, whilst bargain hunters can look to the factory outlets.

◆◆◆
UNION SQUARE
A hub for shoppers at the heart of the city, Union Square is bordered by department stores and hotels, and filled with strollers and pigeons. The plaque at the Geary–Powell entrance tells you that Mayor John White Geary presented

this block to the city for public use as a square in 1850 and that its name derives from the series of violent pro-Union demonstrations held here on the eve of the Civil War. The Victory monument in the middle of the square commemorates George Dewey's naval success over the Spanish in Manila in 1898. Dedicated by President Roosevelt in 1903, it survived the subsequent earthquake. The most famous hotel on the square is the St Francis (originally dating from 1853) whose present building was restored in 1907 and added to in 1972.

The much newer Hyatt hotel on the northeast corner has a plaza featuring a favourite artwork – a fountain sculpted by Ruth Asawa with 41 wraparound bronze friezes that somehow captures the spirit of San Francisco.

If an event is going to take place, more than likely it takes place in Union Square, be it a demonstration or band concert. The most unusual, perhaps, is the annual July Cable Car Bell Ringing competition.

Above: *The all-American snack*
Right: *Union Square, the heart of fashionable downtown*

◆

VINTAGE HOUSES

Saving Victoriana has become a lifelong project for many San Franciscans, and for those interested, driving routes and walking tours have been designed to take in some of the preserved 'gingerbread'-style houses. Of particular note is **Octagon House** at Gough and Union, an 1861 heirloom in Cow Hollow (once the city's dairyland), but it is only open to the public 3 days a month so check for times. The **Haas-Lilienthal House** on Franklin Street dates from 1886 and is the only fully furnished Victorian house open to the public. The **California Historical Society** headquarters, housed in the handsome 1896 brownstone building on Jackson, now contains a museum and reference library. Several other vintage mansions in San Francisco have become small hotels.

◆◆

M H DE YOUNG MEMORIAL MUSEUM

Golden Gate Park.

This, the city's most diversified art museum, has a wealth of masterpieces that include Rubens' *Tribute Money* and El

Greco's *St John the Baptist*. A range of galleries illustrates Western culture from the era of Ancient Greece to the present time, and a large American wing shows off a comprehensive collection of US art. The entrance fee to the museum is waived on the first Wednesday of the month and on Saturdays between 10.00 and 12.00.

SAN FRANCISCO

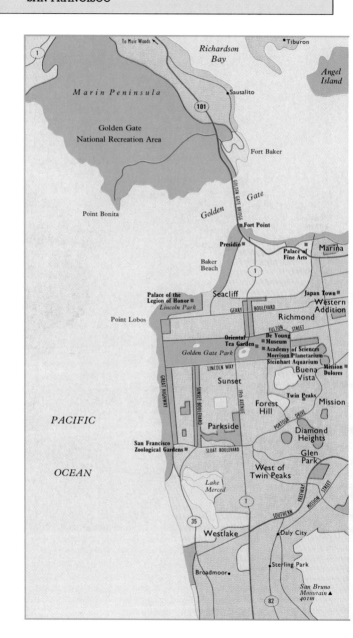

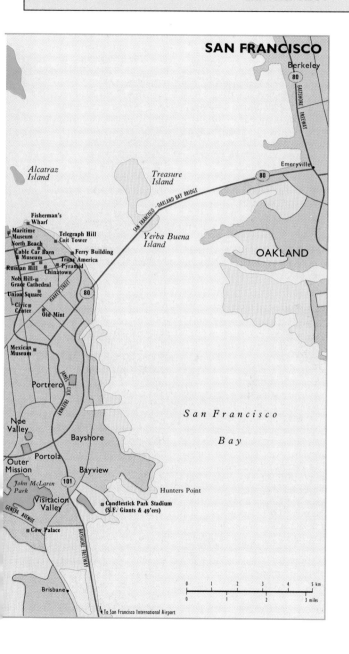

SAN FRANCISCO

Accommodation

There are more than 25,000 guest rooms in San Francisco. The range includes the super-plush, established hotels, newer, smaller, so-called 'boutique hotels' and a recent surge of neighbourhood bed and breakfast accommodation. Three new hotels have recently opened their doors: the 160-room Mandarin Oriental (which occupies the first two and top 11 floors of the 48-storey California Center office tower in the Financial District), the 348-room Portman on Post Street near Union Square (which is affiliated with Hong Kong's Peninsula Group), and Japan Air Lines' 529-room, 25-storey Hotel Nikko at Mason and O'Farrell Streets.

Even newer are the 361-room Park Hyatt on Clay and Battery Streets, Financial District; the 1,500-room San Francisco Marriott, a block from the Moscone Convention Center; and the 92-room/125-residential-suite Aristocrat Hotel at Symphony Plaza. There is so much fine accommodation in the city that it is almost a disservice to list any at all, but favourites are:

The Fairmont, 950 Mason St (tel: (415) 772 5000). A Nob Hill landmark that continues to have the only supper club in the city with top-name entertainers. The original building was supposed to be a home for successful businessman, James Fair, but he died before the mansion was completed in 1894. Today, this highly respected, top-drawer hotel boasts restaurants, a coffee shop, ten lounges and a health club.

The Mark Hopkins, 1 Nob Hill (tel: (415) 392 3434). Named and originally built for a prominent railroad baron, the Mark Hopkins is a splendid Nob Hill landmark. Hopkins died before he could move into his new home which was subsequently destroyed by the 1906 fire. Today's 406-room hotel is home of the legendary 'Top of the Mark' cocktail lounge, first opened in 1939, from where a 50-mile (80km) panoramic view of the city is possible. There is a choice of two restaurants and, of course, 24 hour service.

Sheraton Palace, 2 New Montgomery St (tel: (415) 392 8600). This was America's first truly luxury hotel – hosting Generals like Sheridan, Sherman and Grant. Today, as then, its crown jewel is the Garden Court, where marble columns support a glass roof, lit by crystal chandeliers. This restaurant (one of three) is used for Sunday brunch and dinner buffet – the Palace's trademark, Green Goddess salad, is still on the menu. Guest rooms number 528.

Stanford Court, 905 California St (tel: (415) 989 3500). Yet another Nob Hill historical landmark, this hotel has a European style. Built on the site of the famous Leland Stanford mansion, amenities in its 402 guest rooms unusually include a dictionary! Decorated with many antiques and Carrara marble, the Stanford Court's main

restaurant is Fournou's Ovens.

Recommended inns include:
The Grove Inn, 890 Grove St
(tel: (415) 929 0780). Located in
Alamo Square, this is a turn-of-
the-century Victorian-styled
bed and breakfast
establishment.
The Queen Anne, 1590 Sutter
St (tel: (415) 441 2828). This
1890 building was designed to
be a girls' boarding school. It
is now a 49-room inn offering
complimentary sherry and
concierge service. Rates
include breakfast.
Washington Square Inn, 1660
Stockton St (tel: (415) 981 4220).
A stylishly remodelled 15-room
house – rooms 7 and 8
overlook the square. Breakfast
promises fresh orange juice
and fresh flowers along with
the croissants and coffee.

Restaurants
There are 4,000 to choose from
of many ethnic types and all
price brackets. Some

*A modern backdrop for resplendent
Victorian 'Painted Ladies'*

favourites are:
Blue Fox, 659 Merchant St (tel:
(415) 981 1177) – never cheap
but always respected for its
elegant continental cuisine.
Buena Vista, 2765 Hyde St (tel:
(415) 474 5044) – a Wharf
rendezvous spot that hasn't
changed its looks much from
the 1800s. It became a legend
a couple of decades ago for
the introduction of Irish coffee.
Bountiful breakfasts are served
here, too. Not expensive.
Carnelian Room, Bank of
America Building, 555
California St (tel:
(415) 433 7500) – room with a
view, and what a view!
Cocktails and dinner only
except for Sunday brunches.
Enrico's, 504 Broadway (tel:
(415) 392 6220) – the place to
people-watch in the heart of
North Beach, the city's jazziest
area. And there is live jazz

here, too, on weekends. The fare is international; the prices moderate.

Ernie's, 847 Montgomery St (tel: (415) 397 5969) – award-winning, celebrated and expensive, and that means elegance and *haute cuisine*. It was established in 1934 by Ernie Calesso and Ambrogio Gotti, but don't let this confuse you, the cuisine is French.

Equinox, Hyatt Regency Hotel, 5 Embarcadero Center (tel: (415) 788 1234) – lunch, dinner, cocktails – come for the splendid view from a revolving platform.

Fior d'Italia, 601 Union St (tel: (415) 986 1886) – the city's oldest Italian restaurant, Fior d'Italia has always kept the minestrone flowing. There is a 'Godfather' room and a 'Tony Bennett' room.

Lanzone & Son, Ghirardelli Square, 900 North Point (tel: (415) 771 2880) – founded by Modesto Lanzone from Liguria. The north Italian menu (for lunch or dinner) could well feature delicious *parsoti alla crema di noci* (pasta filled with prosciutto, ricotta and spinach all in a cream sauce with crushed walnuts).

Lehr's Greenhouse, 740 Sutter St (tel: (415) 474 6478) – American cuisine served in a 'garden' setting of lush orchids and ferns. Perhaps just the place for Sunday brunch.

Mama's of San Francisco, 398 Geary St (tel: (415) 788 1004) – theatre district eatery where you can indulge in pancakes topped with berries, omelettes filled with green chilli and sour cream, fresh mushrooms or chicken livers, salads and sandwiches.

Top of the Mark, Mark Hopkins Hotel, 1 Nob Hill (tel: (415) 392 3434) – a 'must' cocktail lounge too celebrated to miss. Recommended for Sunday brunch.

Shopping

From street stalls where artisans sell their own work to major American department stores like Saks and I Magnin, San Francisco has it all. Two of the more interesting department stores are Neiman-Marcus (whose prize feature is its City of Paris dome which city preservationists fought so hard to keep, and won) and the Emporium on Market Street (which also has a grand dome under which one of the world's tallest indoor Christmas trees is suspended each year).

Many goods may be purchased within a four-block radius of Union Square at the hub of the city, but many other shops are housed in complexes. The major ones are:

Anchorage Center, Fisherman's Wharf – a nautical-looking complex within walking distance of both cable cars and crab stands, with Bay viewing points from its decks and outdoor promenades. An array of apparel, leather, jewellery, craft and gift boutiques, art galleries, snack bars and restaurants are all located here. Street performers often entertain in the courtyard.

The Cannery, 2801 Leavenworth – once Del

In San Francisco the lighter side of life is never far away

Monte's cannery overlooking San Francisco Bay, this is now a three-storey complex of more than 50 chic shops, galleries, restaurants and cafés. Look for gourmet foods, rare wines, fine handicrafts and designer fashions and home furnishings. Street entertainers often perform in the courtyard.

Crocker Galleria, near Union Square – modelled after Milan's vast Galleria Vittorio Emmanuele, this tri-level pavilion encompasses over 50 shops and restaurants. Look for designer labels.

Embarcadero Center, between Sacramento and Clay Streets – takes the site of the old waterfront produce market. It is now a complex of 175 shops and restaurants selling just about everything. There is frequent impromptu entertainment.

Ghirardelli Square at the Wharf – for many years a chocolate factory and now a favourite shopping complex with 70 shops and award-winning restaurants. It was the country's first manufacturing complex to be preserved and cleverly renovated into a retail centre. Some of the original chocolate vats and ovens are still in operation on the plaza level of the Clock Tower. It offers frequent free entertainment.

Japan Center, bounded by Post, Geary, Laguna and Fillmore Streets – a 5-acre complex of restaurants, sushi bars, art galleries, bookstores and Oriental gift shops.

Pier 39 on the waterfront – an abandoned cargo pier which has been transformed into a covered market-place with two levels of restaurants and unique shops plus a marina and waterfront park. Good views, and good entertainment at the family amusement area and the San Francisco Experience Theater.

Children

San Francisco attractions of especial interest to the younger age group include the USS *Pampanito*, a 312ft (95m) submarine on display (with commentary about her exploits) at the Wharf's Pier 45. Here, children can look through the periscope and pretend they're Cary Grant. They may well also enjoy clambering about the *Balclutha*, part of the Maritime Museum at Pier 43.

The Zoo is a must – it's a great one! And it's free for those under 15 (if accompanied by an adult). Its newest attractions are the Primate Discovery Center, Koala Crossing and Gorilla World.

Across from the Cannery at the Wharf, the American Carousel Museum lets the under 12's in free. It is a new museum, but its carousels were hand crafted between 1880 and 1920.

Youngsters who feel they would rather ride than look will find a working wooden roundabout at the children's zoo and another in the children's playground in Golden Gate Park. They're both antiques – the one at the outer end of Pier 39 is newer. Depending upon their ages and inclinations, there are many city museums to appeal to children, but a visit to the Tactile Gallery at the Exploratorium (in the Palace of Fine Arts) is a must. As for family theme parks, the most noteworthy nearby are Marine World Africa USA in Vallejo, 30 miles (48km) to the northeast, and Great America in Santa Clara, 45 miles (72km) south.

Watch the world go by on Pier 39

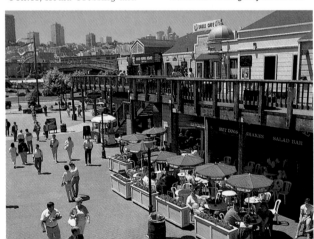

Los Angeles. Two centuries ago this was a tiny pueblo

LOS ANGELES

Where does it start, where does it end? This is the perennial question asked by anyone visiting the urban sprawl of the City of the Angels with its spaghetti network of highways and its municipalities which have burst so much at the seams that they've merged. Los Angeles (or LA as it is commonly known) is a county covering over 4,000 square miles (10,300sq km); it is also a metropolis with a population of around 9 million people. The tiny pueblo of 1781 has boomed and bloomed. Today it is a huge world trade centre; a convention city whose Wilshire Boulevard stretches all the way to Santa Monica. It is almost as difficult to locate downtown Los Angeles, because of its many residential and business pockets – Hollywood, Beverly Hills and Marina del Rey, to name but a few – but it is easy to find where it all began, on Olvera Street. Some people would say that the central point of LA is Hollywood Boulevard where it crosses Vine – a famous corner that has been crossed by innumerable stars. Film stars have helped make LA legendary, living in Bel Air homes, patronising Rodeo Drive shops. They have created new centres for screen activity, such as Universal City and Burbank, and added a magic to doorstep beach resorts like Malibu. The city's elasticity means that it meets the Pacific at such settlements – a string of them that appear to be LA's very own.

Wheels are practically an essential – cars are kings in

LOS ANGELES

Los Angeles. (Indeed, it was 'black gold' – petroleum – which proved so profitable for the city early this century.) Those who don't choose to meet the challenge of driving here can, of course, take organised excursions to places of interest, but should give some thought to their accommodation base. Downtown, for example, is crammed during the daytime, both with commuters and cars, but is likely to be deserted at night. Finding a taxi on the street is difficult so you are recommended to call for one or use the central city shuttle minibus which operates a frequent service between points of interest during office hours. The downtown area is generally considered to incorporate everything around the Civic Center, the business and financial district, and Commercial and Exposition Parks.

Often 'pockets' are cities in their own right, like West Hollywood (Greater Los Angeles' 84th city), which covers part of the flatland section of Hollywood. The latter's hilly section spans places like Nichols and Lauren Canyons. Once a camping ground for the Cahuenga Indians, Hollywood later became a main stop for the Butterfield Stage and was made a city in 1903. Beverly Hills is also a city, designed for the Rodeo Land and Water Company in 1907; Westwood, another.

With mountains, beaches, valleys and a desert to its credit, Los Angeles can justifiably boast it has something for everyone. Wherever your base, you won't be short of accommodation, shops or night-life.

Song-famed MacArthur Park

WHAT TO SEE IN AND AROUND LOS ANGELES

◆◆◆
BEVERLY HILLS
Everyone must have heard of Beverly Hills, where the stars come and go. Organised bus tours take tourists around the stars' homes, pointing out the most famous, though these days many a doctor and lawyer reside in the splendid mansions, as well as the screen celebrities.

The district was originally sheep farms and bean fields. In the late 19th century, it was drilled for oil without success, but in 1900 the Amalgamated Oil Company discovered something just as valuable – water – at Rancho Rodeo de las Aguas (ranch of the gathering of the waters). Hence, company president, Burton Green, planned an exclusive residential community for the site to be called Beverly Hills.

The new development only took off once the Beverly Hills Hotel had been built and began attracting the movie moguls and their entourages. When the Polo Lounge was added in the 1930s, prestige rose even more.

The heart of the community is Rodeo Drive, named for the original Rancho – a premier shopping street for designer label seekers, and star spotters.

Adjoining Beverly Hills is another exclusive community, Bel Air, whose wealthy mansions and estates may just about be glimpsed behind

Famous hideaway for famous people

their secure gates and walls.

◆
CHINATOWN
N Broadway.
This is a quarter to see on foot. It is a typically Oriental sector where you'll find Chinese grocery and gift shops plus restaurants that specialise in Cantonese and Szechuan cuisine.

◆
DESCANSO GARDENS
San Gabriel Valley.
These gardens are particularly famous for their camellias – 100,000 of them in an oak forest setting. Descanso also features extensive rose gardens, a Japanese garden and tea house, and a picnic area. For a small entrance fee, visitors

may walk around at leisure or take a tram tour.

◆
EXPOSITION PARK
Figueroa St at Exposition Blvd.
A 114-acre park containing some of the city's major museums, a 17,000 bush rose garden, the 92,000 seater Los Angeles Memorial Coliseum, and the 16,000 seat indoor Sports Arena.

The **California State Museum of Science and Industry**, here, is an impressive hands-on museum which allows learning to be fun. Subjects explained in surprising ways include electricity, internal combustion and communications – many of the displays are sponsored by major industrial companies. There are also exhibits on health and the human body, and aerospace.

In the **Los Angeles County Museum of Natural History**, major halls are devoted to minerals, palaeontology, living mammals, insects and birds, but there is also a section which relates to Californian history between 1540 and 1940.

◆◆◆
FARMERS MARKET
Fairfax and Third.
During the Depression 18 farmers were allowed to set up stalls here, rent free, to sell their produce directly to the public. Today, there are over 160 stalls in what has become a city landmark, and you can buy fresh food or sample it at take-away kiosks or sit-down cafés. The range is a wide one, from doughnuts to juice and oyster bars, and prices are affordable.

◆◆◆
FOREST LAWN
Glendale.
This amazing cemetery inspired Evelyn Waugh's satire, *The Loved One*, which used the fictitious name 'Whispering Glades'. The highlight is the Great Mausoleum, which houses a number of deceased celebrities including Clark Gable and Jean Harlow. At the Memorial Court of Honor, here, the 'Last Supper' stained-glass window is based on Leonardo da Vinci's famous painting. It is the work of Rosa Moretti, who is said to have had a secret process for making stained glass.

In a special theatre next to the Forest Lawn Museum (where Ghiberti's Paradise Doors have been reproduced), a curtain goes up every half hour to reveal one of the largest paintings on canvas, Jan Styka's *The Crucifixion*. Throughout Forest Lawn there are replicas of renowned statuary, most notably Michelangelo's *David* in the Court of David. Among the churches within the grounds are ones whose designs are based on 10th-century English and 14th-century Scottish examples.

◆◆◆
GRAUMAN'S CHINESE THEATER
Hollywood Blvd.
This prime Hollywood tourist attraction, now called simply Mann's Chinese Theater, was opened in 1927 by showman

Sid Grauman who imported Oriental pillars for it. Whenever a film was premiered here, at what was billed the 'King of Theaters', stars were invited to make their hand or foot imprint in the cement forecourt. Some decided to be more original and made good use of their trademarks – Betty Grable, for example, left an imprint of her leg; Gene Autry, the hoofprints of his beloved horse. Grauman's first theatre was actually *The Egyptian* across the way, built in 1922, and designed as an ancient palace of Thebes. In its heyday, it was the setting for many spectacular and glamorous movie premieres.

◆◆
GRIFFITH PARK
North end of Vermont Ave. Occupying over 4,000 acres in the hills above the city, this park is a favourite recreational area. Once part of the Rancho Los Feliz land grant, it is named for the Welsh newspaperman, Griffith J Griffith, who donated it to Los Angeles in 1896. Its natural mountainside greenery is perfect for picnics and sports like horseback riding and hiking. One of the prettiest areas is Ferndell, planted with all sorts of ferns from around the world.

Gaze at the heavens from the Griffith Observatory on Mount Hollywood

Within the park there are several sites of interest, some, like the **Los Angeles Zoo**, recommended for children. Since it opened in 1966, this zoo has become internationally known for its primates and endangered species. More than 2,000 animals are at home here, grouped according to continent of origin.

Summer performances are given by top entertainers in the **Greek Theater**, a leading amphitheatre, but the park 'highlight' is the **Griffith Observatory**, a distinctive copper-domed structure on top of Mt Hollywood. In its theatre you can easily take a trip to the stars or see a laserium show, whilst from the twin refracting telescope in the Hall of Science, you can take a peek at the heavens on a clear night.

◆
HANCOCK PARK
Wilshire Blvd.

In recreational terms this is a modest park, but Hancock does contain some major museums, including the **Los Angeles County Museum of Art**, which was designed by William Pereira as three pavilions. Most of the permanent collections are in the central Ahmanson Gallery where you will find numerous Impressionist paintings, American art, selections from the Armand Hammer collection of Roman glass and a much-prized collection of Indian and Islamic art pieces. Changing exhibitions are presented in the Frances and Armand Hammer wing;

concerts, lectures and films in the Bing Theater wing. The recent addition to the museum, the Robert O Anderson Building, contains many contemporary paintings including those by Matisse, Picasso and Braque. In the sculpture garden, works on view include those by Moore, Calder and Rodin.

The **George C Page Museum of La Brea Discoveries** houses the fossils recovered from the adjacent La Brea Tar Pits, the largest Pleistocene collection ever found in a single location. More than a million fossils have been gathered, including those of mastodons, giant vultures and sabre-toothed tigers – even the remains of an Ice Age woman. Imaginative displays show the bones and reconstructions.

◆
HERITAGE SQUARE
Homer St.

A 10-acre park where Victorian structures from other neighbourhoods have been brought and restored. Open on weekends, its principal sites (all dating from about 1887) are the Hale House, Palms Depot and Shaw House.

◆◆◆
HOLLYWOOD

These days, it is difficult to define the boundaries of Hollywood, but one thing is for sure, its **Walk of Fame** (both sides of Hollywood Boulevard from Gower to Sycamore, and both sides of Vine Street from Yucca to Sunset) must have seen more feet than practically anywhere else. The 'Walk'

Perhaps the most famous name in America – in letters 30ft (9m) high

encompasses 5 acres of bronze stars set into the pavement as a lasting tribute to those who helped make Hollywood great. There are now over 1,800 of these dedications to noteworthy personalities, and more are added every year.

It was at Sunset Boulevard and Gower Street that films were first made in earnest in 1911, and in a few years there was a host of warehouse-style studios and a bustling industry. Today, the Hollywood glow is not as rosy, though the Paramount and Goldwyn studios still have their headquarters here, and the famed 'Hollywood' sign (on the slopes of Mount Lee in the Hollywood Hills) continues to shine. As a point of trivia, that 30ft (9m) sign was originally designed to advertise a real estate development when it read 'Hollywoodland'.

Also in the hills is the **Hollywood Bowl**, Frank Lloyd Wright's magnificent amphitheatre that seats over 17,000 people. This is the summer home of Los Angeles' Philharmonic Orchestra, which gives classical and pop concerts here. Other performers present jazz, rock, country and folk, too.

To the south of the Bowl, the

Spruce Goose, *on display at Long Beach. This wooden flying boat belonged to Howard Hughes*

Hollywood Studio Museum is housed in the barn used by De Mille for the making of the film *The Squaw Man* and declared a state monument in the 1950s. In the **Hollywood Wax Museum** (on Hollywood Boulevard), anyone who was – or is – anyone in pictures is represented. The museum features its own film theatre where years' worth of Academy Award winners may be viewed, and its own Chamber of Horrors with scenes and props from famous chillers.

Hollywood Memorial Park, on Santa Monica Boulevard, is the last resting place of old-time greats like Tyrone Power, Rudolph Valentino and Cecil B De Mille.

◆
LITTLE TOKYO
San Pedro and First Sts.
The city's Japanese quarter sells and serves, as one might expect, everything Japanese. The focal point of Little Tokyo is the Japanese Village Plaza – an outdoor shopping and dining mall.

◆
LONG BEACH
A city doorstep beach community, this area has recently been revitalised enough to become of considerable tourist interest. It boasts several museums, entertainment facilities and shopping complexes, and every April hosts the Toyota Grand Prix.
Of especial interest is the *Queen Mary*, one of the largest passenger ships ever built, and now permanently moored as a hotel and entertainment/

shopping/museum complex in the harbour at the end of the Long Beach Freeway. A combination ticket enables visitors to explore both the fabled 'Queen' and the *Spruce Goose*, Howard Hughes' wooden flying boat, next door at Pier J. The *Spruce Goose* is purported to be the world's largest plane, with a wingspan longer than a football field and the ability to fit a Boeing 747 under each wing. Inside, life-size models fill the passenger compartment; outside, exhibits show its construction, Howard Hughes memorabilia and a time-travel experience, 'Time Voyager'. The whole thing is encased in an impressive and appropriately large aluminium dome.

◆
LOS ANGELES ARBORETUM
310 N Baldwin Ave, Arcadia. This 127-acre estate features plants from around the world, and its begonias and orchids are particularly noteworthy. Shops and eating facilities can be found on the premises, and another attraction is the ornate Queen Anne cottage, once the home of the property's former owner, silver miner and rancher, Elias Jackson (Lucky) Baldwin.

◆◆
MAGIC MOUNTAIN
A must for children! Run by the Six Flags organisation, this theme park in Valencia may be reached in less than an hour's drive along the Golden State Freeway from Hollywood.
The emphasis throughout the park is on thrill rides, from log flumes to roller-coasters that loop the loop, though there are gentler amusements for the very young, including a mini zoo and Wizard's Village. One admission price pays for all, including puppet shows, dance revues and other live entertainment.

◆
MARINA DEL REY
This beach and watersports centre, with good seafood restaurants and enticing shops, is within easy access of downtown LA. A number of hotels and motels are conveniently situated around the large marina which is located between the international airport and the resort of Santa Monica. Harbour cruises are available for an alternative view of the Marina.

◆◆
MISSIONS
Two Christian Missions survive in the Greater Los Angeles area. San Fernando Rey de Espana, in Mission Hills, was founded by Fermin Francisco de Lasuen in 1797. Since restored, it displays many fine examples of Indian and Spanish architecture and is set in 7 acres of grounds. San Gabriel Arcangel was started by the great founder of California's Missions, Father Junipero Serra, in 1771. The church, which dates from 1805, is famous for its bells, and the museum illustrates early Mission life. San Gabriel Arcangel is at 15151 San Fernando Mission Boulevard.

LOS ANGELES

◆
MUSIC CENTER
1st St and Grand Ave.
For those who enjoy the performing arts, this three-theatre complex is one of the best in town. A resident opera company and philharmonic orchestra are the mainstays of the Dorothy Chandler Pavilion, which also hosts other symphonies, operas, ballets and large musical productions. Plays and smaller musicals are staged in the Ahmanson Theater and the Mark Taper Forum.

◆◆
NBC STUDIO
3000 W Alameda Ave, Burbank.
The only television studio in California to offer public tours. For a small fee you can find out more about sound, lighting and special effects, see behind the scenes, and view yourself on camera. NBC is to be found in Burbank at the inner end of the San Fernando Valley.

◆◆◆
OLD TOWN
If you care to see where Los Angeles began, take yourself to what is now the Pueblo de Los Angeles State Historic Park in the heart of downtown. It was here that 11 families came from Mexico in 1781 to found the city. The best way to tour is on foot from Olvera Street, the city's oldest – a pedestrianised, block-long Mexican market-place lined with craft shops and cafés. A look inside the oldest adobe house, Avila Adobe, is free, as is entry to the city's oldest church fronting the Old Plaza. Pico House (1870) is almost as old and was named for California's last Mexican

The Ahmanson Theater – one of three auditoriums at the Music Center

governor. It was designed to be a prestigious three-storey hotel, and you'll find it on Main Street. The tunnels which led from warehouses to Pico House were once gambling and opium dens.

In the same district, take a look at the Merced Theater, the Sepulveda House and the Pelanconi House and, after the tour, stroll eastwards to Union Station, built in 1939 with a touch of art deco and still in operation.

◆◆
PASADENA

This green and pleasant separate city in the San Gabriel Valley does, in fact, come under the umbrella of Los Angeles and is only 11 miles (17.6km) from downtown. Founded in 1886 and favoured as a winter resort, it is best loved today for its Tournament of Roses Parade and annual Rose Bowl Game. Memorabilia from these events are to be seen in Tournament House and Wrigley Gardens, built by chewing-gum magnate, William Wrigley Jr.

Two important art museums which should not be missed are the Norton Simon Museum of Art and the Huntington. The former has both 20th-century works and works from the pre-Renaissance period. A star attraction is a room full of pictures by Degas, Rembrandt and Renoir. Another of the museum's strong points is its collection of sculptures from India and the Far East. Several British masterpieces, including Gainsborough

paintings, as well as numerous 18th and 19th-century European works have found their way to the **Huntington Library, Art Gallery and Botanical Gardens**. The 207-acre estate used to belong to railway tycoon, Henry Huntington, whose residence is now the art gallery. Other treasures are to be found in the Library – first edition books and manuscripts that include a copy of Chaucer's *Canterbury Tales* and a Shakespeare first folio. Within the grounds are thousands of camellias and roses, not to mention a host of cacti, rare shrubs and trees, and 17th-century Italian statuary.

◆◆
RESORTS

Anyone who likes to combine their city sights with sun and sand, has their choice of oceanside resorts fringing the Pacific, not far from LA. Hermosa Beach and Manhattan Beach are among the lesser known, while Redondo Beach, established by Henry Huntington, is a somewhat industrialised beach resort that offers good fishing. Venice (which never did achieve the developer's plan of looking like Italy's same-name attraction) is a place for people-watching if nothing else.

The two resorts are Malibu and Santa Monica. Malibu found itself a jetset point on the map in the 1920s when the film stars moved into homes here. Even now there is the slight chance of seeing a celebrity

The J Paul Getty Museum, one of the world's richest, in a latter-day 'Roman villa' above Malibu

face, but, beach and surfing apart, the main Malibu attractions are the **J Paul Getty Museum** on the bluffs above the resort, and the **Will Rogers State Historic Park**. The former is without doubt one of the world's richest museums, taking up 10 acres of the 65-acre Getty estate sometimes sarcastically nicknamed 'Pompeii by the Sea'. The building resembles a Roman villa and is filled with prime Roman and Greek antiquities. There are also many exceptional paintings, tapestries and 18th-century French furniture. The Will Rogers State Historic Park was the ranch and home of the 1930s humorous cowboy star of that name. Memorabilia and films of his life can be seen in the visitor centre, and the 137-acre grounds incorporate trails, stables, picnic areas and a polo field.

Santa Monica is a most popular beach centre with wonderful white sand, a range of accommodation in all price brackets, interesting restaurants and direct freeway access from downtown LA. It was already an important city in the 1860s, and was adopted as a favoured resort by the 1870s. Like Malibu, it attracted the stars of the 1930s, some of whose palatial homes still stand. Its major landmark is the (now restored) 1909 pier with its turn-of-the-century carousel, old-fashioned arcade and bumper cars.

♦♦
SOUTHWEST MUSEUM
234 Museum Drive at Marmion Way, Highland Park.
This museum is highly regarded for its expertly researched collection of American Indian relics. Displays cover the anasazi from the southwest, the plains Indians, and those from Mexico and Alaska. Museum founder, Charles Lummis (director of the Los Angeles library in 1907) also donated his own rare books. One of the strongest displays is that of basketry – from every part of the continent west of the Mississippi.

♦♦♦
UNIVERSAL STUDIOS
3900 Lankershim Blvd.
A fun tour on a candy-coloured tram takes visitors through Universal's 420-acre studio lot in Universal City. Regulars along the way include an encounter with 'Jaws', a bridge that tumbles underneath the tram, a flash flood and an alpine avalanche. The latest 'thrill' is an earthquake which collapses the earth under the

tram, fells telephone poles, sparks power cables and crashes a runaway propane truck – all in less than two minutes! Also look for the 'Startrek Adventure', 'Streets of the World', live animal and stuntmen shows, and the chance to be on film yourself. The entrance price isn't cheap, but it's well worth it.

♦
WAYFARERS' CHAPEL
Palos Verdes Drive.
This glass church was designed by the son of the eminent architect Frank Lloyd Wright, and was erected in 1946 in tribute to the 18th-century Swedish theologian Emanuel Swedenborg.

♦
WELLS FARGO HISTORY MUSEUM
Grand Ave.
A recently opened museum showing artefacts, lithographs, photographs and documents about the Old West as they relate to Wells Fargo express and banking company. Entrance is free.

♦
WILLIAM S HART PARK
Newhall Ave.
William Hart is considered the prototype of all Western heroes. He willed his ranch and home to the people of Los Angeles. The museum in the old Hart mansion within the 260-acre park contains mementoes of the actor's career as well as Old West relics; the park features a herd of buffalo and picnic sites among its attractions.

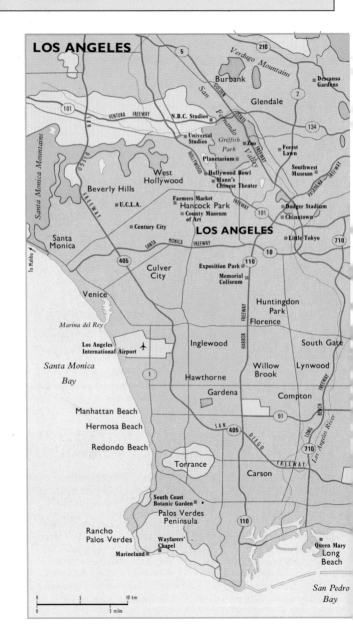

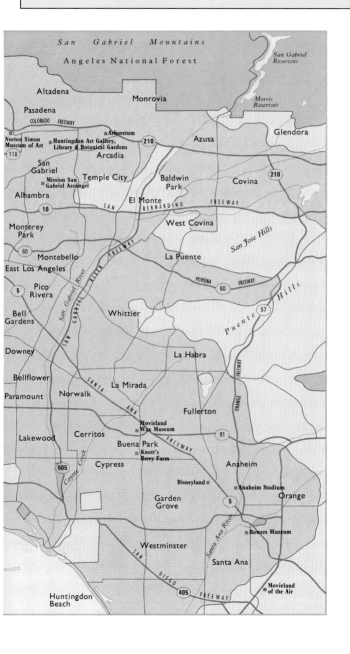

Accommodation

There is an exhaustive supply of hotels, motels and resorts throughout the Greater Los Angeles area so, as mentioned earlier, you are advised to check location first. The following is a selection of top of the range recommendations:
Bel Air Hotel, 701 Stone Canyon Rd (tel: (213) 472 1211). About as exclusive as one can find, this exceptional hostelry only has 92 rooms and suites, all regally appointed. The interior design was re-done in 1982, utilising natural stone and wood-burning fireplaces, and fresh flowers everywhere. The 11 acres of gardens were also improved. The emphasis, as it has always been, is on seclusion.
The Beverly Hills, 9641 Sunset Blvd (tel: (213) 276 2251). The

Choose from nearly 1500 rooms at the space-age Westin Bonaventure

well-heeled have been in love with this 'pink palace' since it opened in 1912. Thanks to 12 acres of tropical gardens, the hotel and its 21 de luxe bungalows are well away from the main road so that privacy is ensured. Not surprisingly, Howard Hughes chose to keep to himself in one of those bungalows. The Coterie restaurant here is plush and pricey, but a salad and a glass of wine in the patio of the famous Polo Lounge is affordable.
Beverly Wilshire, 9500 Wilshire Blvd (tel: (213) 275 4282). A grand dame of a hotel whose Beaux Arts façade was designed in 1928 with a later wing added in

1971. Now a Regent hotel (the company has given it many improvements), it is as handsome and as luxurious as ever.

The Biltmore, 506 S Grand Ave (tel: (213) 624 1011). A de luxe 707-room landmark that has been modernised and restored to its original grandeur. All the rooms feature traditional French furniture and among the 40 suites is one with its own lift and one with a grand piano. The hotel has a new entrance facing Grand Avenue, and the Spanish-styled library overlooking Pershing Square has become Rendezvous Court where breakfast, tea and drinks are served. Other amenities include a health club with pool.

The Westin Bonaventure, 404 S Figueroa St (tel: (213) 624 1000). John Portman designed this hotel comprising five gold-glassed cylindrical towers back in the 1970s and its architecture continues to be admired and well used by business travellers and conventioneers. If you like the large and spectacular this is an excellent (but pricey) downtown base. There are hundreds of guest rooms and eight levels of shops and restaurants. Guests receive complimentary membership of the adjoining LA Racquet Club.

L'Ermitage, 9291 Burton Way (tel: (213) 278 3344). Named in honour of Russia's Imperial Winter Palace in St Petersburg, this luxurious all-suite hotel may not be everyone's cup of tea even if they can afford its rates. It is open only for guests' use, and that includes its elegant restaurant, Café Russe. Many of the suites are split-level and all are beautifully furnished. Service is first class and amenities include a rooftop garden, pool and spa and free chauffeured Rolls for excursions within Beverly Hills. (Le Petit Ermitage nextdoor is more reasonably priced.)

Four Seasons, 300 S Doheny Drive (tel: (213) 273 2222). This newly opened 180-room stylish Beverly Hills property is a sister hotel to London's Inn on the Park and New York's 'The Pierre'. The rooms plus 106 suites are all decorated with antiques; the public rooms with marble and fresh flowers. It's sophisticated and expensive, especially Garden's Restaurant whose dinner menus are particularly eclectic and imaginative. The hotel offers its own terrace pool and café, sauna and jacuzzi, and complimentary limo transport to famous Rodeo Drive.

Hollywood Roosevelt, 7000 Hollywood Blvd (tel: (213) 466 7000). There is a lot of movie history attached to this 410-room Hollywood hotel. It's been a landmark since 1927 when it hosted the first Academy Awards, and for many years was the place to be seen. Errol Flynn, Ernest Hemingway and Shirley Temple are just three of the host of celebrities who have been guests here. Recent renovation has put a fresh gleam on the Spanish colonial lobby with its painted ceiling and the famous Cinegrill restaurant. Facilities include an Olympic-sized pool in the garden.

Restaurants

Downtown, there are fun Mexican restaurants around Olvera Street, Chinese delights in Chinatown, and Japanese delicacies in Little Tokyo. Among the recommendations in the area are:

Mon Kee, 679 N Spring St (tel: (213) 628 6717). A cheerfully crowded and chaotic Chinese restaurant that is notable for its fresh seafood – alive before you order it. Specialities include crab and shrimp in spicy salt.

Oiwake, 511 E 1st St (tel: (213) 628 2678). This is a typical Little Tokyo sushi bar, but one where you can listen to Japanese-style country and western music, and join in, too.

Also well thought of are:
Clifton's Silver Spoon Cafeteria, 515 W 7th St (tel: (213) 485 1726). A good bet for brunch, this elegant but inexpensive cafeteria has a turn-of-the-century setting. Imaginative soups and salads come from the basement Soup Kitchen; other inventive American fare from the Meditation Room.

Cole's Buffet, 118 E 6th St (tel: (213) 622 4090). For years a favourite for a sandwich lunch, and still cheap. It is said the French Dip sandwich was invented here, and other choices include roast beef, corned beef and pastrami.

Tower Restaurant, 1150 S Olive St (tel: (213) 746 1554). A room with a view atop the Transamerica Center. This restaurant is expensive, but worth it with classical French cuisine.

Around the mid Wilshire Boulevard area are:
Center's Fairfax Restaurant, Delicatessen and Bakery, 419 N Fairfax Ave (tel: (213) 651 2030). Probably the largest and liveliest deli on this avenue, it's very Jewish and open 24 hours. It hasn't changed for years, and is still easy on the pocket.

Chasen's, 9039 Beverly Blvd (tel: (213) 271 2168). You'll pay dearly for your chilli or any of the other American basic supper dishes here, the service could be better and no credit cards are accepted. But Ronald Reagan (and a score of other Hollywood customers) have always loved it.

El Cholo, 1121 S Western Ave (tel: (213) 734 2773). Clark Gable used to eat at this classical Mexican place (one of a chain). It has been serving enormous *margaritas* and *tortillas* for 50 years and does have that hacienda atmosphere it emulates.

Pacific Dining Car, 1310 W 6th St (tel: (213) 483 6000). Prime beef and an excellent wine list give this former railway car its deserved reputation as a restaurant. It is open 24 hours.

Perino's, 4101 Wilshire Blvd (tel (213) 487 0000). Elegant, refined, expensive and favoured by local customers who like continental cuisine and near-perfect service. Jacket and tie a must.

There are plenty of interesting restaurants and fast food outlets along Melrose Avenue. But also in Hollywood are:
Butterfield's, 8426 Sunset Blvd (tel: (213) 656 3055). Affordable salads and sandwiches are available here in a pretty patio away from the boulevard's heavy traffic. There is a good choice of wines by the glass.
Columbia Bar & Grill, 1448 N Gower at Sunset Blvd (tel: (213) 461 8800). CBS and other studio types are often to be found lunching here on typically American fare like crab cakes and chilli. Prices are moderate and the airy restaurant has a patio section.
Mischa's, 7561 Sunset Blvd (tel: (213) 874 3467). Russian music and borsch to well after midnight.

Eating is one of the main charms in Beverly Hills. Recommendations include:
The Bistro, 240 N Canon Drive (tel: (213) 273 5633). One of the socialites' gathering places – a place to see and be seen surrounded by *Irma la Douce* décor. Very pricey, but there is superb continental cuisine.
Café Rodeo, 360 N Rodeo Drive (tel: (213) 273 0300). People-watch from the open front here. A moderate price pays for a great salad.
Pastel, Rodeo Collection Shopping Mall (tel: (213) 274 9775). A pretty pink restaurant with its own terrace that serves a simple Californian menu plus a fixed-price French provincial dinner on Thursdays.
La Scala, 9455 Santa Monica Blvd (tel: (213) 275 0579). Still considered one of LA's best restaurants, La Scala attracts the famous with a penchant for Italian fare. Expensive but exquisite pasta and pastries and chicken cacciatore are amongst the offerings.

Shopping
In two words, no shortage. Among the most appealing complexes around town are:
Beverly Center, Beverly Blvd. Three levels of stores, restaurants and cinemas atop four levels of parking slots make up the Beverly Center. This is the location of the Hard Rock Café, the Irvine Ranch Farmers' Market, and a number of boutiques that include Rodier.
Century City Shopping Center, 10250 Little Santa Monica Blvd. An early Los Angeles mall that has been smartened up. It now covers 18 acres and features 100 shops including branches of Bullocks and Broadway. The major attraction is Gelson's market.
El Mercado, 3425 E 1st St. There is a real Mexican flavour at this complex, which is a mixture of a food market, shops and restaurants. Mariachis (strolling Mexican musicians) add to the atmosphere as they play on the mezzanine. Stalls on the main floor sell ingredients to whip up a Mexican meal, and are surrounded by a tortillaria, bakery, snack bars and delis. Crafts can be found in the basement.

LOS ANGELES

Fashion Square, between Woodman and Sazeltine on Riverside Drive, Sherman Oaks – one of the area's early large shopping plazas. Brick-paved outdoor promenades are lined with quality shops, anchored at each end by Bullocks and Broadway department stores.

Fisherman's Village, Marina del Rey – a collection of quaint restaurants and shops next to the marina and cruise departure point for harbour excursions.

Fisherman's Wharf, Redondo Beach – a cluster of unusual shops that line the path to the end of the pier. There are also souvenir stands and stalls selling fresh fish.

Garment District in downtown LA offers all kinds of discount stores for fashions, along Los Angeles Street from 7th Street to Washington Boulevard. Many fashion bargains are on offer in the retail outlets located within the Cooper Building here, and good prices on quality men's suits can be found across the street in Academy Award Clothes.

Japanese Village Plaza Mall, bounded by 1st and 2nd Sts and Central Ave. This cleverly designed complex has white stucco, inset stone paths and ponds, and a traditional fireman's lookout tower as its landmark. A variety of stores and restaurants are to be found here, many concentrating on Japanese food and goods.

La Brea Boulevard, around the junction with Melrose and Wilshire Blvd. Many art galleries are moving into this part of town, adding a smart dimension to what was an odd mixture of car dealers and commercial buildings. Leading galleries include Wenger, Whiteley and Jan Baum.

Los Angeles Mall, Main St, between 1st and Temple Sts. This well-landscaped, multi-level mall was built in the 1970s. It has plenty of room to park, a plaza with shops and restaurants and a pedestrian bridge above Temple Street.

Melrose Avenue, Hollywood. A lively avenue where you can find anything from used clothing to new and radical fashions, trendy design stores and galleries. Parking is difficult especially at weekends when shoppers come in droves. Wear good walking shoes for the 3-mile (5km) stroll from Highland East to Doheny.

Shops in LA can be as eye-catching as their contents

Olvera Street, between Sunset Blvd, Main St, the Plaza and Los Angeles St. This is the heart of downtown LA, with Mexican overtones. Shops and stalls specialise in Mexican crafts and food – made on the spot or imported.

Ports O'Call Village and Whaler's Wharf, San Pedro. A complex at the harbour's edge that combines a re-created New England fishing village and a Mediterranean one – both featuring shops and restaurants; all tend to be boutiquey.

Rodeo Drive, Beverly Hills. Come, if only to window shop at this celebrated purchaser's paradise. Boutiques stock designer labels like Hermes, Ted Lapidus, Ungaro and Louis Vuitton.

Shoreline Village, Long Beach. A cute re-creation of a historical waterfront village with bijou stores and restaurants.

Town and Country Shopping Center, 17200 Ventura Blvd, Encino. Two plazas and complexes on different levels are enhanced by first-class landscaping. A villagey feel to this centre may be helped by the unusual absence of large department stores.

Westside Pavilion at Pico and Westwood Blvds. An indoor modern mall with an airy atrium, though its design also borrows from the arcaded structures of the last century. Between the Nordstrom and May Co department stores are three levels of boutiques offering a mix of clothes, gifts and fast food.

LOS ANGELES

Children

A Universal Studios tour has to be the prime attraction for children staying in Los Angeles, and Howard Hughes' flying boat, *Spruce Goose*, in Long Beach is a firm favourite, too. Downtown, on Main Street, the Children's Museum (the hands-on variety) is specifically designed for youngsters, as is the Long Beach Children's Museum at Long Beach Plaza.

Los Angeles has many museums which will appeal to younger members of the family, often related to the screen stars. The Hollywood Wax Museum, for example, on Hollywood Boulevard, is full of replicas, and you can see how the stars were coiffed and made-up at the Max Factor Beauty Museum on North Highland Avenue. On that same avenue, the Hollywood Studio Museum displays photographs and other exhibits.

Children are sure to appreciate the old carousel on Santa Monica pier – straight out of the film *The Sting* – and may have to be dragged from the Children's Book and Music Center on Santa Monica Boulevard (on some Saturdays there are story hours). Day excursions to Six Flags Magic Mountain theme park and to Disneyland are both possible.

All the fun of the film set. A Universal Studios tour makes an unforgettable day out

The skyline has changed, but San Diego has attracted seafarers for 400 years

SAN DIEGO

There are many reasons for wanting to come to California's birthplace. It is the state's southernmost town, so close to Mexico that popping across the border is considered an afternoon's excursion. It has a near-perfect climate and a premier location between mountains and sea, not to mention a wonderful natural harbour, which completes its appeal to watersport enthusiasts. San Diego's colours are clear, and its lifestyle relaxed, despite its city size. With its heritage, one of America's finest marine parks and a world-famous zoo, plus excellent food and lodging, San Diego can claim to be a true family vacation centre.

A Portuguese explorer, Juan Rodriguez Cabrillo, was the first to sail into the Bay in the 1540s, though it was Sebastian Vizcaino who bestowed the city's name some 60 years later. It was here that Father Junipero Serra founded the very first of the chain of Missions in 1769, and Mexico made it the capital in 1825. Once the Americans had raised their flag, however, San Diego developed less quickly than Los Angeles and San Francisco, and remained villagey until the railroad arrived and the US Navy (who are still here) made it a base. After the last World War, the aerospace industries moved to the area – one of the earliest sophisticated rockets was created here.

In the past few years, sleek mirrored skyscrapers have sprung up downtown alongside the dramatic Horton Plaza shopping centre. The 1980s have also seen a substantial number of new hotels and restaurants, and the reopening of the Old Globe Theater which offers year-round professional theatre.

Reaching the city is as easy as getting around it. By car Los Angeles is only 125 miles (200km) away. The international airport is near downtown and is served by 20 airlines plus. A rail service from LA pulls into the Santa Fe depot downtown. Several bus routes criss-cross the city and operate to the Mexican border; so does the San Diego Trolley. Taxis and rental cars are readily available.

A Sporting City

Since it is a city built around water (with 70 miles (112km) of beaches), San Diego is famous for watersports, particularly year-round ocean fishing. Fitness programmes are also a part of daily life in San Diego, and there are almost 70 golf courses in the county. The local stadium is home for the San Diego Padres baseball team and Clippers basketball team. In winter, whale watching has become an increasingly popular attraction – between mid-December and mid-February some 12,000 grey whales pass the coast here, heading for the warm breeding grounds of Baja California. The viewing is free at the station at Cabrillo National Monument and expeditions can be made for a closer look by boat.

Because Mexico is so close, almost every visitor here makes the trip across the border. You may need a tourist card – if only to shop. There are two crossing points: one at San Ysidro and the second at Otay Mesa. Most people in Tijuana (the Mexican town just over the border) speak some English and most shops will accept US dollars.

Windsurfing in the Bay

WHAT TO SEE IN AND AROUND SAN DIEGO

◆◆◆
BALBOA PARK

This park, the pride of San Diego, has the 1915 Panama–California Exposition to thank for its present structure. Although the land had been set aside by the city in 1868 and an ex-school-teacher was planting trees in 1889, the Moorish and Spanish-style buildings were erected especially for the exhibition and added to for the subsequent 1935 California Pacific International Exposition.

Today, the 1,400 acres encompasses theatres, museums and the zoo. The most prominent landmark is perhaps the 200ft (61m) tall **California Tower** whose 100-bell carillon chimes every 15 minutes. Anyone who has been to Mexico City will be reminded of the famous cathedral there when they look at **The California Building**, though the latter is decorated with statues of those relevant to San Diego's own history, like Cabrillo. Across the way, the small garden is modelled after Spain's Alcazar.

Another replica you'll see is that of Shakespeare's **Globe Theatre**; this one was constructed in 1935. The local outcry was so great at the thought of the playhouse being demolished when the Exposition ended, it was made into a permanent structure, a complex which nowadays features contemporary dramas

Balboa Park: the California Tower from the Alcazar Garden

alongside the Bard's, in three theatres.

Balboa Park also has San Diego's major museums. The handsome tiled Spanish Renaissance villa whose focal point is its staircase and stone atrium, for example, houses the **San Diego Museum of Art**. Its highlights are the superb examples of Spanish art, but its collection also includes other Old Masters, modern American contributions and an Oriental gallery. In the adjacent Italian marble **Timken Art Gallery**, art lovers will find an assortment of paintings and some interesting Russian icons. Remains of this area's earliest inhabitants are housed in the **Museum of Man**, including those of the 3,000-year-old Kumeyaay

Indians and the 5,000-year-old
Del Mar Man. Exhibits showing
the southwest's desert and
marine life are displayed in
the **Natural History Museum**.
By way of contrast, the
Aerospace Museum
concentrates on San Diego's
involvement with aviation
development. Another
favourite venue is the **Reuben
H. Fleet Space Theater and
Science Center** (see under
Children). Smaller specialist
museums are also located in
Balboa: the **Museum of
Photographic Arts**, featuring
changing exhibits by noted
photographers; the **Hall of
Champions**, which pays tribute
to local sportsmen and
athletes; and a museum
housing early Spanish, Indian
and Mexican artefacts.
Balboa is not only about
culture, however. There are
craft shops near the zoo, and
an organ pavilion where
outdoor Sunday concerts are
given. On weekends, street
entertainers are drawn to the
central plaza and horse-drawn
carriages convey visitors up
and down El Prado.

♦
**CORONADO AND
EMBARCADERO**
The Hotel Del Coronado insists
that it is more than mere
rumour that the Duke of
Windsor first met Wallis
Simpson there. It certainly has
hosted presidents and other
celebrities in its time – that's
since the 1880s. Coronado is
virtually an island in the Bay,
but it is attached by a narrow
strip of land called the Silver

Strand, stretching from
Imperial Beach to the
Coronado peninsula.
On the main waterfront, at the
foot of Harbour Drive, Seaport
Village's shops and restaurants
are a pleasant way of spending
some time, or you might watch
the activity from the Harbor
Seafood Mart whilst you eat
some of its produce. Also
along the Embarcadero is the
Maritime Museum, housing
the old steam-powered ferry
Berkeley and the 1863 sailing
ship, *Star of India*.

♦♦
GASLAMP QUARTER
5th Ave.
A 16-block, 38-acre district,

A killer whale – the big attraction at Sea World in Mission Bay Park

is an enormous aquatic park and recreation area where you can charter a fishing boat, swim, sunbathe and picnic. For families, the prime reason for coming to the park is to see **Sea World**, a 135-acre wonderland of marine life. There are aquariums, exhibits, shows and America's largest collection of waterfowl. Among the favourite places to head for are the petting pool (where the animals may be touched), the live shark pool, the sea otter habitat, the walrus pool and the dolphin pool. But tops is the Shamu stadium, recently enlarged, but still home to the park's killer whales – the real star attraction. Here they perform on a grand scale. The complex also incorporates an educational facility called 'Places of Learning'. One not-to-be-missed exhibit, between the shows, is Penguin Encounter, with over 400 Antarctic penguins representing seven species. The park is north of the San Diego River.

recommended for arts and crafts browsers, stretching from Broadway to the waterfront. When entrepreneurial Alonz Horton purchased the property in 1857 it was with the idea of relocating the city centre closer to the ocean. 'New Town', as it was called then, did flourish in the late 19th century as the business hub, but later fell into decline. In 1974 it was revived and its Victorian-era buildings are now mostly art galleries, antique shops and restaurants.

◆◆◆
MISSION BAY PARK
Once a marshland, today, this

◆◆◆
MISSION SAN DIEGO DE ALCALA
10818 San Diego Mission Rd.
This, the first of the Mission chain, was founded in 1769 on Presidio Hill. It was moved to its present location, 6 miles (9.6km) up the valley, in 1774, to take advantage of a good water supply. Inside the Mission, today, is the Father Luis Jayme Museum, which

A Spanish-style façade – one of many reminders that San Diego is on Mexico's doorstep

contains a number of relics of early Mission days, including Father Serra's own handwritten records.

Presidio Hill itself rises above the entrance to Mission Valley and is now a 40-acre landscaped park, and location of the Serra Museum. It is a good vantage point for photographers, looking over the Pacific Ocean, Mission Bay and Mission Valley.

◆◆◆
OLD TOWN

Mason St and San Diego Ave.
Until 1821 Presidio Hill was the San Diego centre, but when it became too crowded settlers moved to the base of the hill. Today, this 12-acre district is a restored historic town to be toured by foot on your own or as part of an organised tour. The setting and atmosphere is of the Mexican and early American periods with buildings dating from 1829 to 1869. Among those to see are the Casa de Estudillo (1830), constructed from logs brought down from the mountains and rawhide to secure the beams, and the Machado/Stewart adobe house.

Casa de Altamirano, a New-England-style frame house, contains a newspaper museum, whilst Seely Stables has Western memorabilia and horse-drawn vehicles. The Whaley House (1856) was the city's first luxury brick home and has been refurnished with antiques and furniture of the period.

Some of the buildings are more than museum pieces, having been turned into gift boutiques and early-California-style restaurants. You'll find several around Squibob Square and at Bazaar del Mundo, as well as in Heritage Park (on the outskirts), where the influence is Victorian.

◆◆
POINT LOMA

This is the location of the Cabrillo National Monument honouring that explorer's 1542

discovery. You can learn everything you need to know at the Visitors' Center and enjoy a marvellous view of San Diego Bay. The best place for whale spotting is the observatory behind the lighthouse. Between December and February each year, thousands of California greys head south from here. The point is 10 miles (16km) west of the city, reached on Catalina Boulevard.

Accommodation
A wide range of hotels, motels and bed and breakfast accommodation is available, but you should choose by area. Downtown/Balboa Park is one area, for example: Mission

Valley (colloquially called Hotel Circle), another. Then there are Harbor Island and Shelter Island, both close to the airport. Among the places recommended are:
Del Coronado, 1500 Orange Ave, Coronado (tel: (619) 522 8000) – a hotel with a certain cachet, located on Coronado Island, linked by causeway to the mainland. It has hosted princes (hence the Prince of Wales Grill), but there are alternative places to eat including an American deli. There are 690 rooms, a pool and tennis on the property.
Half Moon Inn, 2303 Shelter Island Drive (tel: (619) 224 3411) – a smallish hotel with 141 rooms and a

restaurant that features seafood and overlooks the bay.

Hyatt Islandia, 1441 Quivira Blvd (tel: (619) 224 1234) – a 344-room hotel on Mission Bay with comfortable lanai (rooms with patios) and tower rooms. Its coffee garden eating-place has a pleasing setting and the hotel's own marina rents out sailing boats.

The Westgate, 1055 2nd Ave (tel: (619) 238 1818) – a luxurious 212-room hotel in the heart of town across from the Horton Plaza shopping centre. Its Le Fontainebleau French restaurant has won many awards and there is nightly entertainment in the Plaza Lounge.

Selected bed and breakfast accommodation includes:

Balboa Park Inn, 3402 Park Blvd (tel: (619) 298 0823) – conveniently located within walking distance of the Zoo. Some of the 25 rooms have fireplaces and in-room jacuzzis. Local telephone calls are free and breakfast is included in the price.

Coronado Village Inn, 1017 Park Place, Coronado (tel: (619) 435 9934) – 20 units in a European-style resort hotel where you can get budget bed and breakfast. It is within easy reach of the Hotel Del Coronado and the beach.

Heritage Park Inn, 2470 Heritage Park Row (tel: (619) 295 7088) – a restored Queen Anne mansion in the centre of town, with nine rooms. Full breakfasts are served and film classics shown nightly, and evening refreshments and candlelight dinners are available.

Restaurants

Recommendations include:

The Abbey, 2825 5th Ave (tel: (619) 291 4779) – continental cuisine in a historical setting near Balboa Park. Fresh fish is always on the menu and the wine list is extensive.

Anthony's Star of the Sea, Harbor Drive at Ash (tel: (619) 232 7408) – open only for cocktails and dinner, this expensive seafood restaurant is probably still *the* restaurant in San Diego when it comes to fish of all kinds. It also offers a superb view of the Bay and Point Loma.

Casa de Pico, 2754 Calhoun St (tel: (619) 296 3267) – almost a must for lunch, if not for dinner, this Mexican restaurant is in Bazaar del Mundo in the heart of Old Town. The dishes are traditional and reasonably priced and you may choose to eat inside or in the flower-bedecked courtyard.

North China, 5043 N Harbor Drive (tel: (619) 224 3568) – the restaurant is relaxing, the cuisine mostly Mandarin and Szechuan. Look out for the handmade noodles and try one of the bar's speciality Polynesian cocktails.

Shopping

San Diego has both major centres and themed complexes. Among them are:

Bazaar del Mundo, 2754 Calhoun St – in the heart of Old Town, this is a favourite and colourful *mélange* of shops and restaurants, somewhat

Mexican influenced. The Bazaar often hosts free outdoor entertainment.

Fashion Valley, 352 Fashion Valley Rd – a landscaped centre whose 148 shops and six major department stores specialise in high-fashion garments.

Gaslamp Quarter, 410 Island Ave – a 16-block downtown renovated Victorian district where you'll find interesting boutiques, art galleries and restaurants.

Horton Plaza – a modern, innovative, multi-level complex

If you want to get ahead . . . visit one of the city's many department stores

in downtown San Diego. In addition to department stores, there are 150 speciality shops, restaurants, a cinema, theatres, a farmers' market and the San Diego Arts Center. Daily entertainment is a feature.

Marina Village, 1842 Quivira Way – a cluster of boutiques and restaurants located in the basin of Mission Bay.

Mission Valley Center, 1640 Camino del Rio No – the largest most accessible shopping centre where you'll find classy department stores, like Saks, Bullocks and the May Co, as well as 150 speciality shops and restaurants.

The 'wild man' of the jungle – an orang-utan at San Diego Zoo

Old Town Esplanade, 2461 San Diego Ave – Old Town's new centre of interest which simulates a Mexican market-place and sells a wide variety of giftware from around the world.

Seaport Village, 849 W Harbor Drive – a re-created version of an old Californian seaside town on San Diego Bay, with 85 'individual' shops and restaurants plus the more unusual attraction of a restored 1890 carousel.

Squibob Square, 2611 San Diego Ave – a collection of speciality shops with Western-style fronts in Old Town State Park.

Children

The San Diego Zoo has to be tops with any child, in particular the section which specially caters for them with miniature animals at just their height. Located in Balboa Park, the zoo is world-renowned and noted for its many rare and exotic species. Sea World in Mission Bay Park equally delights youngsters. With killer whales starring in their new stadium, other major shows and fascinating exhibits, no one can resent the entrance fee.

The Reuben H Fleet Space Theater and Science Center, in Balboa Park, is another recommendation. Here, a giant OMNIMAX projector, planetarium equipment and specially built screen surrounds the visitor with colour, light and sound. The same building houses a fascinating 'please touch' science centre.

PALM SPRINGS AND THE DESERT COMMUNITIES

Palm Springs is what it has always been – an oasis in the desert. Thanks to an invasion of film stars escaping the hassles of Hollywood in the 1920s and 30s, it has become a very rich oasis, with high property values, glossy shops and many golf courses. In recent years, it has sprouted satellite 'oases' (such as Indian Wells, La Quinta and Rancho Mirage) on its fringes. These are collectively known as the Desert Communities.

It was the Indians who discovered the hot springs in the first place, long before the Spanish arrived in 1774, so perhaps it is appropriate that much of the land today is owned by their descendants. Those who live here, though, aren't short of cash either: past and present inhabitants include Bob Hope, Gerald Ford, Chaplin's son and Sonny Buono. Walter Annenberg's estate (where the Duke and Duchess of York stayed during their 1988 visit) is so vast it has its own golf course.

The weather is the Desert's biggest attraction, especially the winter temperatures, usually in the 70s or 80s. The Santa Rosa and San Jacinto mountains protect Palm Springs from the sea coast's clouds and fog and there's no industry to pollute the air. Vegetation which grows naturally is used cleverly for landscaping – mesquite trees, a profusion of oleanders, a carpet of purple verbena – but local residents do give their olive trees a 'poodle cut' to prevent a mess when the trees scatter their fruit. Local residents are also particular about signs – anything that is

An oasis for the well-heeled, Palm Springs lives up to its name

garish, such as neon, is forbidden, so Palm Springs' McDonald's appears very sedate without its drive-up windows and its giant yellow arches. (Such sign laws, however, do not apply to the surrounding communities). Palm Springs and the Desert Communities are practically synonymous with golf – everywhere you look there's a course. Among the more unusual are La Quinta citrus course (so called because it is surrounded by citrus trees), and the course nicknamed 'golf on the rocks' because it looks like Alcatraz in the desert, surrounded by water, against a mountain backdrop. It costs $200,000 (each year) to grass seed each course and it takes a million gallons of water a day to keep it green.

Water, of course, comes from the mountains when the snow melts, and there are 26 wells in the area. Indian Wells, for example, was so named because the Indians had wells close to the ground's surface.

Golf Crazy!

Visiting and resident celebrities play golf; others come to watch the tournaments whose winners walk away with hefty prizes. Palm Springs is so golf crazy it even holds an annual golf-cart parade! But there is other sport, too – acres of tennis-courts, riding stables, hiking trails – plus the newest fashion, ballooning. Several companies offer 1 hour flights, usually just after sunrise or just before sunset when desert weather conditions are at their

best for this kind of flying.
In the film *Lost Horizons*, Palm Springs was used as the locality of 'Shangri-La' – tranquil, beautiful, majestic, inaccessible. It suits the place, although these days the desert oasis is easy to reach by road or air from Los Angeles.

WHAT TO SEE IN AND AROUND PALM SPRINGS

◆◆◆
AERIAL TRAMWAY

This is Palm Springs' major attraction, operating year-round from the 2,643ft-high (805m) Valley Station to the mountain lodge level of Mt San Jacinto State Park and Wilderness, at 8,516ft (2,595m). In summer, hikers use it, in winter the skiers come. 'Crocker's Dream', a 22-minute film depicting the tram's history, is screened throughout the day for free in the lower level theatre of the Mountain Station. There is a ride charge though to reach the top where there is a restaurant and a bar. It was electrical engineer, Francis Crocker, in the 1930s, who insisted that a tramway could be constructed in rugged Chino Canyon to allow people to retreat from excessive summer heat, but his dream wasn't fulfilled until 1963.

Outdoor enthusiasts today can use (in summer) as many and as much as they like of the 54 miles (87km) of hiking trails in San Jacinto State Park. The really keen might opt for the 5½-mile (9km) trek to the peak; the less intrepid can stick to

The Joshua Tree National Monument – a vast area northeast of Palm Springs

the one-mile-long (1.6km) nature walk through pleasant Long Valley, where a permanent ranger station is located. Throughout the Wilderness area, there are five designated camping grounds; there are also short guided trail rides and longer guided walks.

In winter, the area is perfect for cross-country skiers who can rent equipment and take instruction at the Nordi Ski Center, open from mid-November to mid-April. The more adventurous can rent snowshoes for treks into the Wilderness and even snow camp.

Valley Station is on Tramway Road, 3 miles (5km) southwest of Highway 111.

◆◆
INDIAN CANYONS

S Palm Canyon Drive.

For a nominal fee, this Indian-owned land may be explored at leisure, by car, on horseback or as part of an organised expedition. There are many natural beauty spots, often used as film backdrops. One of the best known is Palm Canyon. It extends for 15 miles (24km) through a series of rock gorges and minor canyons, but may be reached by an easy footpath. For equestrians, the scenic trail to Andreas Canyon is recommended.

The nearest of the canyons to the city of Palm Springs is Tahquitz – a foot trail which starts within city limits and leads to Tahquitz Falls.

PALM SPRINGS

◆◆◆
LIVING DESERT
47-900 Portola Ave, Palm Desert.

This enormous slice of desert may be reached in a 20-minute drive from the city and is both a wildlife park and a botanical garden. Animals in the habitat include bighorn sheep and coyotes, and there are also hundreds of exotic desert plants on display. Self-guided nature trails as well as picnic sites are added features which make this a popular excursion destination.

◆◆
MOORTEN'S BOTANICAL GARDEN
1701 S Palm Canyon Drive.
More than 2,000 varieties of

desert plant growing here prove that the desert is not that harsh. For a small fee, visitors can take self-guided trails which will lead them past some exciting desert sights, including cacti from all over the world, a palm oasis and a wildlife feeding area.

◆◆
PALM SPRINGS DESERT MUSEUM
101 Museum Drive.
Against the backdrop of Mt San Jacinto, this 20-acre facility features dioramas and displays that relate to the locality, as well as changing exhibitions and science programmes. On the same site, the Annenberg Theater features a host of top-name performers.

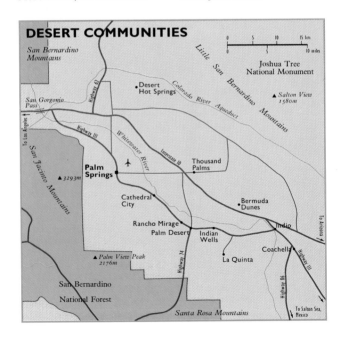

DESERT COMMUNITIES

The Desert Communities

◆
CATHEDRAL CITY
From a mere 'bedroom' community for neighbouring Palm Springs, Cathedral City has achieved its own identity, though it is still being developed. Its accommodation (which includes motels) is more reasonably priced than the other communities.

◆
DESERT HOT SPRINGS
A 10-minute drive from Aerial Tramway, this community has its own lodgings, restaurants and shops, and sport facilities that include three public golf courses. It also has its own museum – Cabot's Old Indian Pueblo – which houses a collection of early days relics, including a buffalo leather shield from the Custer battlefield.

◆
INDIO
One of the oldest communities in the Coachella Valley, Indio is set amid date palms. The first National Date Festival was held here in 1921 and is repeated annually each February. Another claim to fame is reflected in its title 'Winter Polo Capital of the West'. The Eldorado Polo Club here certainly attracts many of the world's best players.

◆
PALM DESERT
A plush valley community, Palm Desert is home to the hotel chain Marriott's amazing resort and spa (for which sand was imported from Israel and for which the girls steering the lagoon boats received instruction from the US coastguards!). The McCallum Theater for the Performing Arts, part of the Bob Hope Cultural Center, and the multi-million dollar town-centre mall and exclusive El Paseo shops are other attractions here.

◆
LA QUINTA
La Quinta probably has more golf holes per square mile than any other city. Here is the Western home of American golf – PGA West – whose championship courses have been designed by Pete Dye, Jack Nicklaus and Arnold Palmer, and are used for prestigious tournaments such as The Skins Game and the PGA Club Professional Championship.
Famous La Quinta Hotel was an exclusive retreat in the 1920s and has hosted many screen celebrities. When the community was incorporated as a city in 1982, ceremonies were held on this hotel's lawn.

◆
RANCHO MIRAGE
A prestigious place to live and stay. There are ritzy hotels like the Ritz-Carlton and Mission Hills resort, and ritzy houses like that belonging to Frank Sinatra (which has a model railway in its grounds).

Accommodation
Most of the desert hotels are true American resorts and there has been an increasing number of very fine ones since

Gene Autry financed his first hostelry. Among the most lavish are:

Hyatt Grand Champions,
44-600 Indian Wells Lane, Indian Wells (tel: (619) 341 1000). Nearly 300 of the 340 guest rooms are split-level parlour suites, but there are also 20 garden villas which have private butler service and their own spa pool. Recreational facilities include a health and fitness centre, four pools and 12 tennis courts.

Marriott's Desert Springs Resort and Spa,
74-855 Country Club Drive, Palm Desert (tel: (619) 341 2211). This mega resort spreads itself over 400 acres and has 891 guest rooms. The design incorporates lagoons via which guests are ferried from point to point in small canopied boats, if they don't choose to walk.

Other major resort features include a man-made beach, three swimming pools, two 18-hole golf courses, 16-tennis courts and a fully equipped health spa.

Mission Hills Resort Hotel,
71-333 Dinah Shore Drive, Rancho Mirage (tel: (619) 328 5955). More intimate, this hotel's 248 guest rooms are housed in low Moroccan-style buildings with either balcony or terrace views of the golf course or mountains.

La Quinta Hotel Golf and Tennis Resort,
49-499 Eisenhower Drive, La Quinta (tel: (619) 564 4111). Legendary since 1926, La Quinta's 269 guest rooms are in Spanish-style cottages scattered over 26 acres. This hotel is particularly noted for its buffet lunches and its tennis facilities – 30 hard courts, six grass courts and three clay.

Restaurants
Between Cathedral City and Palm Desert, in the Rancho Mirage district, is an area known as 'Restaurant Row'. Among the many establishments worth trying are:

Las Casuelas Nuevas, 70050 Highway 111 (tel: (714) 328 8844). It's large, it's Mexican and it's reasonable. Decorated with hanging plants, a fountain, tall Mexican chairs and oak-topped tables, this is the very place for a 'house plate' – *enchilada*, *tamale*, *taco*, *chilli con carne* and beans or rice. Accompany your meal with popular Mexican beers or *margaritas*.

The Wilde Goose, 67-938 Highway 111 (tel: (619) 328 5775). This restaurant has won many awards for its creative cuisine. If you're not ready for roast goose, buffalo meat, venison or the even more exotic wild boar or alligator, there's always roast duck prepared five different ways, prime rib and beef Wellington. Rustic decor, speciality drinks and entrée prices that start under $20 add to the charm.

Shopping
El Paseo in Palm Desert is a must. Among the speciality stores are:

Air Dreams, 73-900 El Paseo – this place combines art with fashion. It's an art studio that

Marriott's Desert Springs provide a luxurious oasis in the desert

specialises in limited-edition, hand-painted designs on T-shirts and dresses. All clothes are washable and epitomise the Desert lifestyle.
Chama, 73-405 El Paseo – Chama features distinctive contemporary clothing and unusual jewellery and accessories. Look for natural fabrics and designer labels like Laise Adzer.
Richard Danskin Galleries, 73-920 El Paseo – here you can buy realistic countryside and horse paintings by Danskin. Also look for desert scenes by local artists.
Diane Freis, 73-111 El Paseo – well-known American designer, Diane Freis' Desert shop features limited-edition dresses in lightweight polyester georgette as well as fashion scarves.
Knits Etc, 73-425 El Paseo – this store stocks a wide range of unusual knitwear, often one-of-a-kind. Another feature is handpainted art on knitted belts, handbags and jewellery, as well as handpainted needlepoint.

Children
Recommended for youngsters is a visit to the Oasis Water Park on the Gene Autry Trail, open from March to September. There is an admission charge but children under four can come for free. Major features are the huge wave pool where they can surf or raft, and the freefall and speed slide.

NAPA VALLEY

Just north of San Francisco, Napa Valley is best known for wine. There are countless vineyards which may be visited, and their end products sampled. Before there were grapes, there was cattle ranching, then walnuts, then prunes. Now, in addition to the 118 plus wineries, there are 2,000 guest rooms in the area, many restaurants, sport facilities and spas.

Mt St Helena, at 4,344ft (1,324m), dominates the landscape and is thought to be an extinct cinder cone, a type of volcano. When it erupted millions of years ago, it uprooted gigantic redwoods and petrified them with its hot ash. Nowadays you can see the result in the Petrified Forest, which leads from Calistoga over the hill to Santa Rosa.

One of the most popular ways of overseeing the region is by balloon. Mist, of course, can prevent a flight, but if the weather is right, there is no better idea than floating lazily, high over the vines. Several companies offer the experience, which usually includes a glass of champagne. Alternatively, from the Calistoga Soaring Center, glider flights are available.

Vineyards thrive in the Mediterranean climate of the sheltered, south-facing Napa Valley

WHAT TO SEE IN THE NAPA VALLEY

◆◆◆
CALISTOGA

At the northern end of the Napa Valley, Calistoga is a noted spa area, first discovered by the Wappo Indians. However, it was a Mormon, Sam Brannan, who recognised that the natural qualities of the hot-water geysers and mineral springs would attract visitors. He gave the town its name in 1859 in

honour of both the state and New York's Saratoga. Today, a number of places offer therapeutic treatments including steam baths and massages.

Calistoga's main attraction lies 2 miles (3km) out of town. The geyser 'Old Faithful' is fed by an underground river that heats up to well over boiling point every 40 minutes before spouting water in the air as high as 60ft (18m).

◆◆◆
ST HELENA

Robert Louis Stevenson lived in this small town 10 miles (16km) south of Calistoga, and wrote of his experiences in *Silverado Squatters*. Entrance to the Silverado Museum here is free. The museum contains memorabilia of the writer's life and work, including first editions, original manuscripts and photographs.

Just north of the town an 1846 water mill has been preserved in the Bale Grist Mill State Historic Park, whilst in Bothe-Napa Valley State Park, there are 10 miles (16km) of hiking trails up steep hillsides, leading to groves of redwoods.

WINERIES

Napa Valley has become a respected wine region the world over and has so many wineries it would take days to cover them all. The following offer tours and tastings: Beaulieu (St Helena), Beringer (St Helena), Domaine Chandon (Yountville), Christian Bros (St Helena), Folie a Deux (St Helena), Franciscan (Rutherford), Freemark Abbey (St Helena), Inglenook (Rutherford), Hanns Kornell (St Helena), Charles Krug (St Helena), Louis M Martini (St Helena), Joseph Matthews (Napa), Merlion (St Helena), Robert Mondavi (Oakville), Monticello (Napa), Sterling (Calistoga).

Especially recommended visits are:

Beaulieu – the visitor centre incorporates a small theatre where you can watch an audio-visual presentation on the vineyard's history plus a general introduction to wine-making.

Beringer – the family home, the Rhine House, built in 1877, typifies German architecture. (Many of the first wine-makers were of German descent.) Part of the building houses a visitor and wine-tasting centre, and regular tours are given through the limestone caves that were built in the late 1800s by Chinese labourers, to provide the ideal environment in which to age the wine.

Domaine Chandon – the tour here is somewhat unique for Napa since it covers the making of sparkling wine.

Christian Brothers – the main building, Greystone, was built by Chinese labourers in 1889,

Over 100 varieties of grape are grown in this part of California

using stone from local quarries. This winery has one of the largest collections of oak cooperage in the United States, and an unusual antique corkscrew collection.

Inglenook – in one of the ageing cellars, a wine library shows visitors a collection of Inglenook wines dating back to 1882. Artefacts, bottles, documents and photographs tracing the history of Napa wine-making from the 1800s can be seen in the winery's Centennial Museum.

Robert Mondavi – very good guided tours here give a

complete overview of the wine-making process.

Sterling – this is located on a hilltop and reached by cable car. There are marvellous views of the valley and visitors may take themselves on a self-guided tour.

◆◆
YOUNTVILLE

Yountville was named for George Calvert Yount, the first white settler in the Napa Valley. He fell in love with the place in 1831 and, with the help of local Indians, constructed a Kentucky blockhouse (a small fortified building) and mill. In 1855, a surveyor was commissioned to lay out the city. By the time Gottlieb Groezinger established his winery and distillery in 1870 (now a shopping and restaurant complex), Yountville was a thriving farming community. Today, it is still a pleasantly rural tourist attraction.

Accommodation

This region of California is rather special in as much as it boasts a large number of interesting inns and bed and breakfast establishments. Among them are:

Coombs' Residence, 720 Seminary St, Napa (tel: (707) 257 0789). This two-storey house was built in 1852 and is furnished with antiques. A delightful but small place with only four units, it provides hotel comforts like large bath towels as well as a swimming pool and jacuzzi.

The Pink Mansion, 1415 Foothill Blvd, Calistoga (tel:

(707) 942 0558.) Dating from Victorian times, the Pink Mansion features a formal living room with fireplace as well as a dining room and games room for guests' use. Private bathrooms, large breakfasts and afternoon wine and cheese are offered by the proprietors.

Vintage Inn, 6541 Washington St, Yountville (tel: (707) 944 1112). A rustic 80-room establishment that is actually more like a hotel than an inn.

Wine Way Inn, 1019 Foothill Blvd, Calistoga (tel: (707) 942 0680). A friendly house with six named and prettily decorated guest rooms.

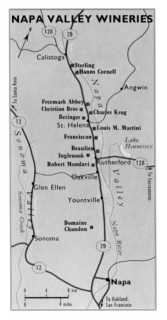

Restaurants
California Café Bar and Grill, 6795 Washington St, Yountville (tel: (707) 944 2330) – features Californian cuisine with a kick, including Mesquite grilled seafood, Cajun specialities, and pastas.

Domaine Chandon, California Drive at Highway 29, Yountville (tel: (707) 944 2893) – an elegant, very French restaurant that is part of the winery. Dishes frequently use wine in their preparation and are designed to complement Domaine Chandon's wine.

The French Laundry, Washington St at Creek St (tel: (707) 944 2429) – open only for fixed-price dinner. Dining is leisurely in this old stone building and if you care to wander around the garden between courses, feel free to do so.

Shopping
In the small towns of this area, expect to find country craft and antique shops as well as shops selling just about everything. An interesting complex is Vintage 1870 in Yountville, once a winery. Among the boutiques here are:

The Chutney Kitchen – for lunch or purchases of home-made Californian chutneys.

The Country Mouse – a cottage shop featuring dried flowers and collectables.

Fruit of the Vine – look for Napa Valley silk-screen and embroidered sportswear.

Groezinger Wine Company – the place to stock up on Californian wines and sample them in the wine bar.

SONOMA VALLEY/RUSSIAN RIVER

The tree-clad shoreline of Lake Sonoma

Like neighbouring Napa, the county of Sonoma has a wealth of vineyards – located in the Valley and along the Russian River. Padre Jose Altimira planted the first vines at the Mission of San Francisco Solano and, when this Mission was closed, General Mariano Vallejo planted vines for his own use. For several years, he competed with Agoston Haraszthy, a Hungarian count who created California's oldest winery, Buena Vista, and who chose Sonoma for its climate, perfect for viticulture. Sonoma was also the place where the first state flag of California was raised, in June 1846. At that time Mexico was governing the territory and had ordered American settlers out. In order to hasten American occupancy, a small band of rebels took Vallejo prisoner and raised their own home-made flag – a piece of unbleached muslin with a red stripe, a painted grizzly bear and a star, and the words 'California Republic' – in the plaza of Sonoma pueblo. A month later, once the American navy had captured the then capital, Monterey, and claimed California for the US, the 'Bear Flag' was replaced with the 'Stars and Stripes'.

WHAT TO SEE IN THE SONOMA VALLEY/RUSSIAN RIVER

◆◆

GLEN ELLEN

A hamlet just a few miles west of Sonoma, Glen Ellen was the home of author, Jack London, who wrote more than 50 books including *Valley of the Moon*. Others of his books, like *The Sea Wolf* and *The Call of the Wild*, have become American classics, but it was *Valley of the Moon* that brought fame to this region; the name 'Sonoma' is said to be of Indian origin, meaning 'many moons'.

As a memorial to London, the Jack London State Historic Park was established in 1959 where the author's famous 'Beauty Ranch' takes up 800 acres. His widow, Charmain, built 'The House of Happy Walls' in 1919, and this houses many mementoes of London's richly varied life. This park is popular with equestrians – a 3-mile (5km) trail leads to the summit of Sonoma Mountain.

◆◆

LACHRYMA MONTIS

This is the name of General Vallejo's 20-acre estate, which he moved to after he left his adobe home, Casa Grande, on Sonoma's plaza.

The notable architectural features of this redwood-frame house are its large gothic windows and carved ornamental eaves. The general and his family lived here until 1890.

◆◆◆

SONOMA

The birthplace of the county, Sonoma, has a central plaza which was laid out by General Vallejo in 1835, surrounded by the largest collection of Mexican-era adobe buildings north of Monterey.

Of prime importance is the San Francisco Solano Mission, founded in 1823. The padres' quarters in a long, low wing next to the present adobe church are Sonoma's most historic building (1825); the existing church dates from 1840. Also bordering the plaza is Vallejo's first home, Casa Grande, built in 1836. What is now the Toscano Hotel was an 1850s general store and

The padres' quarters at Sonoma, built only two years after the Mission was founded in 1823

library. Vasquez House, now a historical museum, was once the home of General Joseph Hooker, a Civil War general with a penchant for young girls of questionable virtue (hence the word 'hooker').

Sonoma is also famous for Sonoma Jack, a type of high-moisture cheese. It has been manufactured in Sonoma since 1931 and continues to be a traditional food item. 'Jack' cheeses were originally made on Monterey farms, pioneered by Scottish merchant, David Jacks. Nowadays, all flavours are available from onions or garlic to caraway and hot peppers.

WINERIES

Recommended vineyards in the Sonoma Valley with tours and tastings are:

Buena Vista (Sonoma) – California's oldest premier winery. Self-guided tours through the 1857 cellars, a tasting room with an antique press, and lovely grounds in which to picnic make this number one.

Chateau St Jean (Kenwood) – wines made here include sparkling. Self-guided tours are available.

Gloria Ferrer (Sonoma) – dedicated to sparkling wine, this vineyard has recently achieved more widespread recognition.

Gundlach Bundschu (Sonoma) – visitors follow self-guided tours, but there are plenty of knowledgeable personnel around to give the answers. There is also a hiking trail with a view of the valley.

Sebastiani (Sonoma) – a respected family winery with an award-winning product.

Russian River Wine Road recommendations are:

Clos du Bois (Healdsburg) – sample 12 wines from the Alexander and Dry Creek valleys.

Foppiano Vineyards (Healdsburg) – family-owned since 1896.

Johnson's Alexander Valley (Healdsburg) – unique tasting room contains a 1920s theatre pipe organ.

F Korbel (Guerneville) – famous champagne cellars.

Landmark (Windsor) – the main vineyard building is an old Spanish villa surrounded by extensive lawns and gardens. The winery's major product is chardonnay.

Simi (Healdsburg) – noted for its state-of-the-art equipment.

Sotoyome (Healdsburg) – the name is derived from the Old Rancho Sotoyome; where there were once ranches is now the heart of the county's wine country.

Accommodation

The Sonoma Valley and Russian River region is liberally scattered with inns and bed and breakfast establishments. Among them are:

Camellia Inn, 211 North St, Healdsburg (tel: (707) 433 8182). An Italianate Victorian mansion furnished with antiques, twin marble fireplaces and an impressively ornate mahogany dining room.

Campbell Ranch Inn, 1475 Canyon Rd, Geyserville (tel: (707) 857 3476). Set in 35 acres on top of a hill with vineyard views, this inn's four comfortable guest rooms feature king-size beds.

Sonoma Valley Inn, 550 2nd St W, Sonoma (tel: (707) 938 9200). More of a hotel with 75 rooms, and your choice of wood-burning fireplaces or private jacuzzis, plus kitchenettes.

Vintner's Inn, 4350 Barnes Rd, Santa Rosa (tel: (707) 575 7350). A 44-room country inn surrounded by a working vineyard.

Restaurants

Catelli's the Rex, Geyserville Ave, Geyserville (tel: (707) 894 3337) – home-cooked Italian food in Russian River wine country, at reasonable prices.

Depot Hotel, 241 1st St W, Sonoma (tel: (707) 938 2980) – a country inn with an inexpensive North Italian menu and a wine list that highlights local wineries.

The Sonoma Cheese Factory, 2 Spain St, Sonoma (tel: (707) 996 1000) – a great place for lunch – sandwiches and salads feature all kinds of Sonoma Jack cheese. You can also watch this cheese being made and buy some to take out.

Topolo's, 5700 Gravenstein Highway N, Forestville (tel: (707) 887 1562) – this family-owned Russian River Vineyards restaurant is in a turn-of-the-century farmhouse. Specialities are Greek, and portions are hefty.

Shopping

A fun place to shop is the Historic Railroad Square in Santa Rosa, site of the arrival of the first Santa Rosa & North Pacific train in 1870. Among the stores which can be visited here are:

Blue Goose, 60 W 6th St – filled with turn-of-the-century American oak items.

California Silk & Dried, 100 4th St – silk and preserved flowers and foliage.

Sweet Potato, 129 4th St – they call themselves a 20th-century dime store!

Whistlestop Antiques, 130 4th St – two floors of antiques and collectables.

WHAT TO SEE ELSEWHERE IN CALIFORNIA

'Great Moments of US History' – a Disneyland interpretation

◆◆◆
ANAHEIM

The prime reason for coming to Anaheim is because it is a centre of major family attractions (including Disneyland). This part of Orange County is easily reached from Los Angeles (via the Santa Ana Freeway) in a rental car or by way of an organised coach excursion. The last part of Anaheim's name means 'home' in German, and was given by settlers who came here with vine cuttings in 1857 – until the late 1800s this was the state's wine capital. When a blight devastated the vineyards, the grape growers turned to oranges, but it was Walt Disney's choice of the site for a new and different theme park that made Anaheim bloom and become a name on everyone's lips. The city literally grew up around the 76 acres of Magic Kingdom, and it is now Orange County's largest city. Anaheim's buildings are impressive, no more so than the **Convention Center**, which not only caters to business people but frequently stages concerts, ice shows, etc. Also impressive is the **Stadium**. It cost $21 million to build, seats 70,000, and is the local home of the California Angels baseball team.

Then there are the shops – in modern multi-storey centres or cleverly designed villagey complexes. Try the Anaheim Plaza or Seaports of the Pacific. The latter features waterfront restaurants and live country music on the wharf, an international bazaar, an off-road raceway, a video game centre and variety shows like

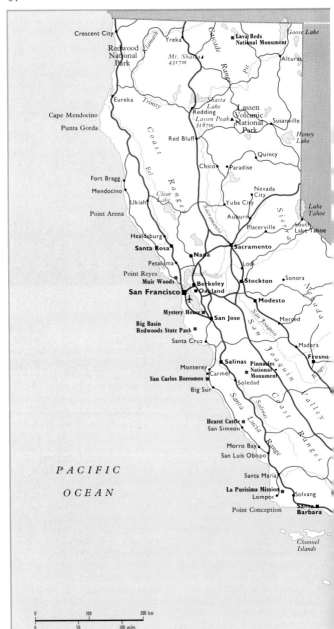

CALIFORNIA

OREGON   IDAHO

Points of Interest
International Airport
Principal Highway
Other Highway

NEVADA

UTAH

Mono Lake
Yosemite
National Park
    •Mammoth Lakes
  ■ **Devils Postpile**
        •Bishop
Kings Canyon
National Park
                ■ **Scotty's Castle**
                ■ **Ubehebe Crater**
Sequoia
National
Park   •Independence
              Mt. Whitney
            ▲ *4418m*
  •Visalia   *Owens*
              Lake   **Devil's**
                      Golf Course■
    •Porterville   *Telescope Peak* ▲
                      3368m
                              Death Valley ~*-86m*
•Delano

  Bakersfield   •Ridgecrest

        Mojave
              ■ **Ghost Town of Calico**
                Barstow
      •Lancaster   *Desert*   **Needles**   ARIZONA
                                    Colorado
  ■ **Magic Mountain**   *Sonora*
•Ventura   **Pasadena**   *Desert*
Oxnard   **San**
              Bernardino
Los Angeles■ **Riverside** **Palm Springs**■
                                •Indio
Long Beach■ **Anaheim**   •Blythe
        Newport   **Riverside**
        Beach   Borrego
Santa   Springs•   *Salton Sea*
Catalina Oceanside•
Island   Encinitas• Escondido•   *Imperial Valley*
        Del Mar•   •Brawley
            San Diego■   El Centro•   *Gila*

MEXICO

WHAT TO SEE

the Polynesian Fantasy and Dancing Waters.

Nor does the city lack places to stay, suited to family budgets. Many are at the edge of **Disneyland** and this, of course, is the attraction that adults and children alike want to see. Since the park opened in 1955, it has never looked back, adding new shows and rides all the time. The lands are still 'themed' – Adventureland, Bear Country, Fantasyland, Frontierland, Main Street, New Orleans Square and Tomorrowland – each with its own special enticements. Favourite rides, such as 'Pirates of the Caribbean', 'Haunted Mansion', 'Jungle Cruise' and 'Space Mountain', continue to

operate, and there is constant live entertainment (big bands, jazz, etc) as well as parades and fireworks. Disneyland recently introduced 'Star Tours', the three-dimensional space musical 'Captain EO', and 'Splash Mountain'. The latter features one of the world's longest and fastest flume drops – over 50ft (15m) high and reaching 40mph (64kph), as well as 100 'audio animatronic' characters from *Song of the South* placed in various areas throughout the ride to help tell a story. One admission fee covers all. While in the Anaheim area you should combine a visit to

A far cry from fruit-growing – Knott's Berry Farm

Disneyland with the nearby attractions of the town of **Buena Park**. The most notable theme park here is **Knott's Berry Farm**, a success story bar none. Walter and Cordelia Knott came to Orange County in 1920 from San Luis Obispo (where they had been sharecroppers) and started a berry farm on 20 acres of land. They sold fruit and jams from a roadside stand and later, chicken dinners. Today, the complex covers 150 acres and features a wide range of rides and entertainments. The five themed areas are Old West Ghost Town, Fiesta Village, Roaring 20's, Knott's Airfield and Camp Snoopy, and popular rides include the 'Calico Mine Trip' and 'Sky Jump'. The latest ride is 'Kingdom of the Dinosaurs', taking you back through time to prehistoric days. As at Disneyland, live bands perform here, and dolphin shows are presented in Marine Stadium.One entrance fee pays for all. Just opened is a sixth themed area, Wild Water Wilderness, which includes an exhilarating 'Wild Water Rapids' thrill ride.

One block from the park, **Medieval Times** offers medieval banquets in a European-style castle where knights joust and fence.

◆

BORREGO SPRINGS
This desert oasis, 90 miles (145km) northeast of San Diego, is the best base for visiting the **Anza-Borrego Desert State Park** since it boasts plenty of motels in all price brackets. Most of the park's 600,000 acres are as rugged as they were in Spanish times, so ranger guided walks or tours are recommended. From Borrego Springs itself, it is possible to take a 40-mile (64km) circular trip, stopping at Font's Point to look at the Badlands with its chasm gashed from towering granite walls, and at Palm Canyon where hundreds of palms grow.

◆◆◆
CARMEL
Carmel is really little more than a village by the sea, albeit a charming arty one, referred to by Americans as 'quaint'. Named by the Spanish in honour of the Carmelite friars, it is situated at the southern entrance point to a 17-mile (27km) Scenic Drive and is the perfect beauty spot for a honeymoon. You won't find skyscrapers or convention hotels here, but instead accommodation is usually in an inn and restaurants are cosily intimate. Shops, too, tend to be of the boutique, speciality and art gallery kind. Set on its sandy crescent on the Monterey Peninsula, backed by cypress-covered hills, Carmel is reminiscent of European coastal communities. A few miles along the coast, **Point Lobos** was what Robert Louis Stevenson called 'the most beautiful meeting of land and sea on earth'. It is a pleasure to walk through this state reserve and possibly swim in a cove sheltered by Monterey cypress.

WHAT TO SEE

◆
CATALINA ISLAND
Situated 26 miles (42km) off the coast from Long Beach, this resort island used to be the property of William Wrigley Jr. It is noted for clear water and warm sandy beaches, appealing to sunbathers and snorkelers alike. From the pleasure pier at Avalon, the capital, glass-bottomed boats and flying-fish boats leave on tour. Public transport operates to the island's interior, but no cars are allowed on the island.

Those who wish to stay here have a choice of resort hotels and inns, including the last home of novelist Zane Grey (now a guest house), and the Wrigley Mansion. Catalina can also easily be reached as a day's excursion from Long Beach by boat or air or on the recently introduced hydrofoil service.

Ubehebe Crater is one of many extraordinary landforms in Death Valley, which was once the floor of an inland sea

◆◆
DEATH VALLEY

Adjoining Nevada, Death Valley National Monument is America's third largest, covering 3,000 square miles (7,770sq km), and contains the hottest spot in the US. During the Gold Rush, a party of prospectors (the 'forty-niners') were stuck in this hot, low, dry place, hence the valley's name, but there are springs and streams here and there is life: the pupfish or desert sardine has learnt to live and flourish with high temperatures. So do desert mammals and reptiles. And though Death Valley isn't green, it has plenty of other colours: Golden Canyon shines gold in the sunlight, Mustard Canyon is ochre tinted, Mosaic Canyon's grey rocks contain pebbles in many different hues, and Red Cathedral, a natural clay amphitheatre, is indeed red. Take Artists' Palette Drive to enjoy some of the best of this colour.

The highlight is Dante's View, 5,474ft (1,668m) above sea-level, a point from which you can see almost all of Death Valley. Below is Badwater, 282ft (86m) below sea-level, and the lowest point in the US. Above are the Panamint Mountains and the Telescope Peak, over 11,000ft (3,000m) high. And in the distance, the second highest point in the United States, Mt Whitney, shimmers under its 14,494ft-high (4,417m) snowcap. Nature's oddities abound in Death Valley, once the floor of an inland sea, as you can tell from sections of sand dunes. A bed of salt crystals is also evidence of the place's maritime past – an area of odd salt formations which remained after the sea evaporated have been named 'Gnome's Workshop'. There are man-made oddities, too, like the ghost town of Skidoo, once a mining centre, or Scotty's Castle, an unfinished Spanish–Moorish palace built in a remote canyon by a flamboyant Californian character, Walter Scott. Because of its temperatures, Death Valley's main tourist season is from mid-autumn to mid-spring.

◆◆
FRESNO

This lively city is the banking, financial and agricultural centre of the San Joaquin Valley. Almost right in the middle of California, it provides plenty to see and do and plenty of hotel chain accommodation. One of its focal points is **Roeding Park** where 167 acres are planted with a variety of trees and shrubs including roses and camellias. The park is the setting for Fresno's zoo – with over 700 animals and birds and a computer-operated reptile house. In the city you'll also find Storyland, a children's fantasy area, with picnic sites and fishing lakes. Another city park for a summer day is **Woodward Park**, on the San Joaquin River, with its bird sanctuary, fitness course, children's playground and Japanese garden.

WHAT TO SEE

Fresno has several worthwhile museums; **Discovery Center** is a favourite with all ages. Highlights of this hands-on science museum are the exhibits of whisper cones, laser phone, electronic sound tree and a room of native Indian artefacts. At the **Metropolitan Museum of Art, History and Science** you can see a sizeable collection of Old Masters, still-life and *trompe l'oeil* paintings, as well as photographs by Ansel Adams.

◆
LAGUNA BEACH

A typically Californian beach town clad with palms and eucalyptus, Laguna (to the south of LA) takes its name from the word for lakes. (It has two freshwater lagoons.) The place is so picturesque, the atmosphere so leisurely, that it has always been an artists' colony. Not surprisingly, you'll find boutiques, craft shops, art galleries, festivals and art-related events here.

◆◆◆
LA JOLLA

It looks like the French Riviera, this jewel of a resort reached in a 15-minute drive from San Diego. La Jolla's postcard prettiness (along with its weather) has attracted the artistic for many years.

The blue expanse of Lake Tahoe is fringed by three National Forests

The Indians called this place 'La hoya', meaning cave – several caves can be seen from the cliff-top overlooking the most popular swimming beach, La Jolla Cove. You can go into the largest cave if you wish, through the Cave Curiosity Shop at the northern end of the Coast Boulevard and down 133 steps.

La Jolla Cove appeals to skin-divers as it is part of the San Diego–La Jolla Underwater Park, an underwater conservation area, but only experienced divers are allowed to explore it. Winter migration of the whales is best seen from Whale Point. Water and marine life are more than just for fun in this resort, which is also a research centre, being the home of the Salk Institute and the Scripps Institution of Oceanography. At the latter there are 22 large tanks housing sea mammals, crustaceans, fish and marine plants. Visitors may observe the effects of tidal activity via an artificial tide pool. There is motel accommodation here, but the inns are more atmospheric; there are also many cosy bars, pavement cafés and first-class restaurants.

♦♦♦
LAKE TAHOE

Lake Tahoe has the distinction of being two-thirds in California and one-third in Nevada and is an excellent year-round resort area. This 12 by 22-mile (19 by 35km) alpine lake was discovered by pioneer John Fremont in 1844 on his journey from Oregon to California. It was just as central to the migration of the native Washoe Indians before the Gold Rush fortune hunters came along.

For scenic beauty, you could not do better since Tahoe lies in a basin between the main Sierra Nevada and the eastern offshoot of the Carson range, surrounded by the national forests of Eldorado, Tahoe and Toiyabe.

The region boasts the finest accommodation and restaurants in the High Sierra – 100 eating places, 16,000 rooms. It also boasts an incredible amount of sunshine and an equally incredible amount of winter snow – nearly 18ft (5.5m). Whatever the time of year, many activities are possible. From spring to autumn, hiking, biking, horse-back riding and ballooning are popular. In summer, sailing, water-skiing, rafting and fishing are ideal – you can rent a boat from one of the marinas or take a paddle-boat cruise that includes a meal. For winter skiers, Lake Tahoe is a west coast paradise: the Tahoe Basin is renowned as a world-class downhill skiing destination, but in addition it has thousands of acres available for cross-country skiing. It's also scenic and there are 212 ski lifts and tows. The Lake Tahoe Visitor Center on Taylor Creek will give you information about trails, flora and fauna. Artefacts from the region's earliest days are on display at the Lake Tahoe Historical Society Museum on

WHAT TO SEE

Volcanic Mount Lassen broods over a sparkling, lake-strewn landscape

Highway 50, and you can also get details of the self-guided car tour of 20 landmarks in the South Tahoe area here. Those who seek city lodging should head for Tahoe City on the north side of the lake.

◆◆
LASSEN VOLCANIC NATIONAL PARK

Some say it is a miniature Yellowstone, this small national park located 47 miles (75km) east of Redding, off Highway 44 in northern California. Mt Lassen, after a long sleep, erupted 300 times between 1914 and 1917. This snow-covered dome at the southern tip of the Cascades is the focal point of the park but there are numerous other peaks here, 50 wilderness lakes and acres of forests. Mt Lassen's bubbling mud pools, hot springs, cinder cones and the steamy holes known as fumeroles are an exciting reminder that it is still an active volcano, but the recent restful decades have turned this into a safe (though still adventurous) area for hikers and skiers.

Headquarters for the park are in Mineral on State Highway 36. The area's county seat is at Susanville, and this could be a good accommodation base. The second largest natural lake located within California, Eagle Lake, is only 20 miles (32km) from the town, and is noted for its fishing and sailing possibilities.

Within the park, numerous hiking trails lead to the thermal areas. The 2½-mile (4km) Lassen Peak Trail leads to the top but an easier way takes you to Bumpass Hell, which is the largest hot-springs area –

Little Hot Springs, Big Boiler, Steam Engine and the Sulphur Works are all nearby. The park's eastern section is the most rugged but it may be reached by pack-horse trips which leave from Summit Lake. The resort area is around Manzamota lake (only open in summer) where there are campsites and lodges available for travellers.

◆
MAMMOTH LAKES
This four-season holiday area lies in a 9,000ft (2,700m) deep, lake-strewn basin below Mammoth Mountain. The town of Mammoth Lakes itself is a resort base for excursions into the area, with a range of places to dine and lodge. It is a convenient base for drives to Yosemite National Park, some 30 miles (48km) northwest, or Inyo National Forest, a little further to the east. Two local lakes of interest are Convict Lake and man-made Crowley Lake, stocked with fish. Rainbow Falls is the site where the San Joaquin River tumbles 140ft (42m) over lava ledges, and nearby Devil's Postpile National Monument, created 900,000 years ago by hot lava, has giant columns resembling organ pipes.
Mammoth Lakes is a challenging territory for hikers, backpackers and mountain climbers, but most of all attracts the skiers. The region is one of America's largest ski areas, offering one of the longest seasons, sometimes as far into the year as July! You'll find 29 lifts, 150

trails, 30,000ft (9,000m) of vertical runs, cross-country skiing, ice-skating on Convict Lake and wind-skiing in the meadows – and plenty of mountain lodges, too.

◆◆
MENDOCINO
Often called the 'New England of the West Coast', this village in northern California is favoured by artists and is frequently used as a location for films and television shows. Its Cape Cod style of architecture is due to the timber men who settled here from Maine in the mid-19th century. In addition to the quaint houses, some of which have been converted to bed and breakfast inns, there are unusual shops and art galleries, and cosy restaurants. The Mendocino coast, stretching from the Gualala River to Point No Pass, is a most attractive one, a draw for artists, fishermen and wine-growers. Along the southern part of Highway 1, several picturesque coastal villages are located, including Anchor Bay, Little River, Albion and Point Arena.

◆◆◆
MONTEREY
This scenic port is a must on anyone's itinerary. When Sebastian Vizcaino set foot on the Monterey Peninsula in 1602, its destiny was sealed – Monterey became one of the first and most successful settlements in California; indeed it was the capital until the American flag was raised in 1846.

WHAT TO SEE

Always dependent upon the sea, for a long time Monterey was a whalers' retreat. **Fisherman's Wharf**, built in 1848, served as a pier for trading schooners from around the Horn, and was the focal point for the whaling and subsequent sardine industries. Today, it is a tourist's delight, lined with seafood restaurants and speciality shops.

More shops and restaurants are found along **Cannery Row**, whose renaissance is due to the fame of John Steinbeck's book *Cannery Row*. Between 1921 and 1946, Monterey was a sardine capital, with 16 canneries packing over 240,000 tons of sardines each year. When the sardines disappeared, the 'Row', as Steinbeck knew it, died, and only in later years has tourism revived it.

At the western end of the Row, the **Monterey Bay Aquarium** allows close-up viewing of the Bay's underwater world. The 177,000-square-foot (16,000sq m) aquarium provides homes for over 5,500 sea creatures from sharks to otters. Then there's the 28ft (8.5m) deep tank through which you can see a functioning kelp forest, and another tank which re-creates the deep reefs and contains sharks, bat rays and other open-ocean fish.

A number of Monterey's historic buildings have been incorporated in the **State Historic Park**, staffed by guides year-round. The old Custom House, for example, is the state's oldest government building, and California's first theatre was built here, adobe-style, as a boarding house and saloon.

Although the city is not neon-lit, it is lively, with a highly regarded September jazz festival and 70 other annual special events taking place within the peninsula. There are plenty of hotels and golf courses, but perhaps the greatest attraction is the **17-mile Drive**. This scenic route takes you around the peninsula from Pacific Grove to Carmel's Mission (see separate entry) and back to Monterey, passing Seal Rock, Cypress Point, Spyglass Hill and Pebble Beach.

The Pacific coast near Monterey

◆◆ MT PALOMAR

From the visitors' gallery in Palomar Observatory, you can view the huge telescope which has a range of one billion (US) light-years. It utilises mirrors instead of a lens and therefore acts as a giant camera – photographs taken from it are on display in the exhibit hall. Mount Palomar is 40 miles (64m) northeast of San Diego.

◆ OAKLAND

From San Francisco, the bridge is more obvious than the community of Oakland, despite the fact that the latter is the Bay's largest rail and port city. The Oakland–San

Francisco Bay Bridge is an engineering marvel, spanning 8½ miles (13.6km) between Rincon Hill in San Francisco and the toll plaza in Oakland. At some point you are almost bound to cross it.

The city of Oakland is, of course, commuter territory, but it is also the site of an enormous saltwater tidal lake – **Lake Merritt**. Canoe or row on it, jog or bike around it – the lake is also a national duck refuge. At the northern end of Lakeside Park, **Children's Fairyland** has replicas of favourite nursery rhymes, some with live pets – a theme area said to have inspired Walt Disney for his own first theme park.

At the foot of Broadway on Oakland Estuary, **Jack London's Waterfront** is the best place for food and entertainment. The author frequented the First and Last Chance Saloon here, now a restored attraction on the square.

◆ PETALUMA

You may well pass through this little town that held the title 'Egg Basket of the World' on your way to or from Napa and Sonoma's wine country. (Its title derives from the fact that it once produced a vast amount of poultry and eggs.) If you can't resist oddities, stop – you'll like it. Petaluma trivia, for example, tells us it is the only town in North America with a commercial snail ranch; that actor Lloyd Bridges was a star basketball player at its high school; that the world's first and only drug store for chickens was located here; and that Winners' Circle Ranch, breeder of horses under 32 inches (81cm) high, is the only miniature horse farm west of the Mississippi open to the public!

All that apart, you may care to wander around the downtown historic buildings, some of them of typical Victorian style. They were designed with iron fronts in the belief that this would prevent fire. It didn't, but 26 of the old buildings do survive.

◆◆

REDWOOD NATIONAL PARK

Within this national park, right in the north of California, are three state parks: Jedediah Smith, Del Norte Coast and Prairie Creek. In the Jedediah park, there are 18 memorial redwood groves, including the Frank Stout grove whose 340ft (104m) Stout Tree is the greatest attraction. Camping facilities and a beach can be found along the Smith River. There are several campsites in various sections of the Del Norte park and, of the trails which lead from them, the 2-mile (3km) Trestle Loop Trail behind the Red Alder camping ground, is thought to be best. Prairie Creek park has a host of redwoods and, thanks to generous rainfall, is green with other foliage besides, so that Fern Canyon's walls are emerald with mosses and lichens. Herds of elk are visible in the meadows of the Madison Grant section of this park and the best trail is said to be Revelation.

The whole park covers 106,000 acres, with 8 miles (13km) of coastal roads and 100 miles (160km) of trails leading to redwood groves. A favourite route is the Avenue of the Giants, which begins in Phillipsville and ends at Jordan Creek. For 33 miles (53km) this route runs along the Eel River, popular with campers and fishing fans. A shuttle bus service operates from the visitor centre in Orick to Tall Trees Grove, where the tallest known tree, over 367ft (112m), may be seen.

◆

RIVERSIDE

Racing fans know Riverside well, for its international raceway is the site of such events as the Budweiser 400. In earlier days this city, in inland southern California, was a rich centre for navel oranges – in 1895 there were 20,000 acres of them. Reminders of that early wealth remain visible in its elaborate Victorian architecture. **Heritage House** is a particularly fine example, built in 1892 at a cost of $10,000, and beautifully restored. Another landmark is **Mission Inn**, originally a 12-room adobe structure of 1875, gradually added to and embellished to contain over a million dollars' worth of antiques including Tiffany windows.

Opposite the old City Hall, the Renaissance-style **Municipal Museum** houses a large collection of Indian artefacts

Relaxing by the Smith River in Jedediah Smith Redwood State Park

and exhibits of the citrus industry's early days. Agricultural traditions are kept alive at the **Botanical Gardens**, 37 acres of hilly terrain whose emphasis is on dry-climate plants – over 2,000 species, many spring blooming. For the children, **Castle Park** is a 28-acre family park whose focal point is a three-level arcade crammed with games.

◆◆
SACRAMENTO

California's state capital has something for everyone: history, waterfront activity, elegant restaurants. It started to grow when Swiss-born John Sutter built a fort at the confluence of the American and Sacramento Rivers in 1839. Today, the restored structure is **Sutter's Fort State Historic Park** and it shows how things looked when this was central California's first outpost of civilisation. On special Living History days, guides in period costume re-enact life as it was in the 1840s. Adjacent, the **State Indian Museum** displays aspects of Indian life and culture from dug-out canoes to burial grounds.

Old Town, along the Sacramento River, comprises 28 acres of Gold Rush era buildings, cobblestone streets and wooden pavements, where one can take a trip back in time the easy way. This is how the area looked in the 1860s, though there wouldn't have been the cafés and restaurants, boutiques and gift shops that you'll find here now. Among the restored structures are a one-room school, an assay office, a post office and the Old Eagle Theatre, built in 1849 and still staging shows. Ardent train spotters will find an exceptionally comprehensive railway museum in Old Town – the **California State Railroad Museum** features 21 locomotives and innumerable historic railway relics. Most famous from the bygone age is

Forty acres of parkland surround the State Capitol in Sacramento. The elegantly proportioned building dates from the 1860s

the *Southern Pacific 4294* steam locomotive, weighing over a million pounds. Others to look for include Lucius Beebe's lavish private travelling rail car and the 1860s *Governor Stanford* steam locomotive.

Sacramento used to be the end of the line for the Pony Express. This western terminus, now the **B F Hastings Museum**, shows exhibits of this special delivery service. Gold is the highlight display at the **Sacramento History Center**, a reconstructed version of the 1854 City Hall and Waterworks

building. Nor has Old Town's waterfront been forgotten. It was a busy supply centre in the 1850s with hundreds of paddle-wheelers, like the *Delta King* (now permanently docked), plying their trade along the river. Enjoy the experience on a replica paddle-wheeler, such as the *Matthew McKinley*, one of several to offer daily sightseeing cruises.

Not far from the Old Town sector, **Governor's Mansion** has been home to 13 state governors, including Ronald Reagan. It's open now as a showplace of 19th-century opulence. The West's oldest art museum, the **Crocker Art Museum**, is located on O Street and is most noted for a major collection of Old Master drawings.

For pure recreation, take to the rivers – both the Sacramento and American can be fished or rafted. Youngsters will find a children's themed area, playground and amusement centre as well as the city's zoo in **William Land Park**, or you could take them along to **Gibson Ranch County Park**, in existence since the 1870s, where they are free to feed the domestic animals. If they're very energetic, head for **Waterworld USA** on Exposition Boulevard – 14 acres of wet and wild attractions, including high-speed slides and activity pools, should keep them amused.

WHAT TO SEE

◆
SALINAS

In the heart of a productive farming belt, a 20-minute drive from Monterey, Salinas was John Steinbeck's birthplace. His house, currently a restaurant and gift shop, is part of what has been designated Old Town – nine square blocks in the heart of downtown. Some of his original manuscripts and other memorabilia can be seen in the nearby John Steinbeck Library. His Salinas experiences led to such novels as *East of Eden* and *Of Mice and Men*.

◆
SAN JOSÉ

From 1849 to 1851, San José was the state capital, but the 20th-century claim of this city to the south of San Francisco is as a leading centre for technology. Microchips apart, the most bizarre place to visit is **The Winchester Mystery House**. Eccentric Sarah Winchester (heiress to the famous rifle fortune) was so convinced that she would live as long as she kept adding to her mansion, that carpenters were busy for 38 years installing windows, doors (often opening onto walls), fireplaces and staircases (often leading to nowhere). She couldn't keep the spirits at bay, but the eerie 160-room house is worth the tour price. Visitors can guide themselves around the gardens and outbuildings, and can also see the Winchester Firearms and Antique Products Museums.

◆◆
SAN JUAN CAPISTRANO

This city, between Los Angeles and San Diego, is most famous for its Mission, founded in 1776 and the seventh in the chain established by Father Serra. Take yourself round the Serra Chapel and the ruins of the original church, to which it is said the famous swallows return each year on 19 March. The city, named for St John Capistran, which has grown round the Mission, has become a popular resort readily accessible to Disneyland. Situated on rolling hills between the mountains and the sea, San Juan Capistrano is filled with lovely old adobe buildings and has an Amtrak terminal that is a restored 1895 Santa Fe railway station.

◆◆◆
SAN SIMEON

A crowning glory – or is it folly – of the Central Coast is Hearst Castle or, as it has since become, Hearst San Simeon State Historic Monument. It is the 'fantasy' estate of newspaper magnate William Randolph Hearst, born into a wealthy San Francisco family and given his own newspaper to run when aged only 24. He was the man who said 'Pleasure is worth what you can afford to pay for it'. San Simeon glitters atop a knoll overlooking that great scenic route, Highway 1. 'La Cuesta Encantada' or the Enchanted Hill was where Hearst

A tycoon's dream come true – Hearst Castle at San Simeon

entertained people from all walks of life. His family donated the estate to California in 1957, 6 years after his death. The man who expanded his business into a vast publishing empire collected *objets d'art* from around the world to fill his 'castle', a combination of Italian, Spanish, Moorish and French architecture that took nearly 30 years to complete. Inside one of the high-ceilinged rooms, there are life-size statues of saints and 16th-century silk banners; in another, priceless tapestries and marble medallions, each weighing a ton. Outside, there are sculpture gardens, Greco-Roman pools and marble terraces.

Because the estate is so big – comprising 123 acres of grounds – visitors have the choice of four separate tours of the house and gardens.

◆
SANTA ANA

The government seat of Orange County, Santa Ana may be reached from Los Angeles via the Santa Ana Freeway and is a good base for touring the county. Its own major tourist attraction is the **Bowers Museum**, a hacienda-style structure that houses an outstanding and very large collection of West Coast Indian and pre-Columbian art. The **Movieland of the Air Museum** has an original theme for its displays: it traces the history of aviation by way of those aircraft made famous in films, such as the 'Sopwith Camel' and the Fokker Tripe 'Jenny'.

◆◆
SANTA BARBARA

This is a famous Spanish-influenced beach resort with distinctive red-tile-roofed buildings and Moorish doorways. A 1925 law has helped preserve Santa Barbara's historic legacy and many of its fine old structures have been lovingly restored. One of those is the **County Courthouse**. It takes up a whole city block and is considered one of the greatest public buildings in the West. Inside, there are handpainted frescos, wrought-iron chandeliers, historic exhibits and Tunisian tiles; outside, a sculptured façade and sunken gardens. From its 70ft (21m) clock-tower you can see across the city.

The courthouse is a key site

The 'Queen of Missions' at Santa Barbara was founded in 1786

along what Santa Barbara calls its 'Red Tile Tour', which will also take you past **El Presidio**. The guard's house and Canedo Adobe are part of the original Spanish fort on a site blessed by Father Serra in 1782, but the padre's quarters and chapels are reconstructions. It was Spanish conquistador, Sebastian Vizcaino who sailed into Santa Barbara's bay in 1603 and named the port for the saint whose birthday it was that day. By 1786, the presidio was the focal point of the Spanish stronghold whose Mission was so beautiful it was called 'Queen of Missions'.

If you are here in August, you will see the Plaza de la Guerra turned into a colourful market-place for the annual celebration of the Old Spanish Days Fiesta. El Paseo's shopping arcade, built around the Guerra family's 1827 adobe home, is redolent of Spain with its speciality shops, art galleries and dining courtyard. Another fine place to shop and eat is Stearns Wharf at the foot of State Street; from here you can overlook miles of superb beaches.

Treasures from this historic city's past are on view in the **Historical Museum and Casa de Covarrubias** on de la Guerra Street, whilst much of the display area of the **Santa Barbara Museum of Natural History** is devoted to native Indian artefacts. Also in the vicinity, in a wooded area bounded by Mission Creek, is an observatory and planetarium.

The beach – and there are 30 miles (48km) of it – is still the number one reason for selecting Santa Barbara as a base. Family-priced motels include Best Westerns, Vagabond and TraveLodge; sports include sailing, scuba diving, surfing and swimming. To the north of town, along Highway 154, vineyards (over 22 in the county) produce premier Californian wines – you can taste them at several establishments.

◆
SANTA CRUZ

Santa Cruz is a seaside resort 90 minutes' drive south from San Francisco, whose 1904 boardwalk or promenade was the first attraction of its kind on the West Coast. The boardwalk has since been rebuilt, but its amusement park, arcade of games and old-fashioned carousel continue to operate and delight the visitors. On the municipal pier, adjacent, you'll find a market, seafood restaurants and the departure point for bay cruise ferries.

Abundant marine life can be seen in the nearby **Natural Bridges State Park** area which is noted for its sandstone arch. Not far from here, at the **Long Marine Laboratory and Marine Aquarium** (part of the University of California), there are tidepool aquariums, an 85ft (26m) skeleton of a blue whale and the chance to look in the back door at current research. Regional natural history exhibits are displayed at the **Santa Cruz City Museum**, and in the octagonal landmark that was the Hall of Records and is now the **Santa Cruz County Historical Museum**, county history is recorded in exhibits. More unusual is the **Santa Cruz Lighthouse's Surfing Museum**.

Like the other coastal communities, Santa Cruz is big on watersports: pier fishing, sailing from the small yacht harbour, powered craft, and deep-sea fishing charters.

A popular excursion will take you to Felton in the Santa Cruz mountains where a 1920s train will take you on a 2½-hour trip from the redwoods at Roaring Camp back to the seashore at Santa Cruz.

WHAT TO SEE

♦♦

SEQUOIA AND KINGS CANYON NATIONAL PARKS

These adjacent parks form the gateway to the southern Sierras. Dominating the beauty of the natural scenery that stretches from the foothills of the San Joaquin Valley to the Sierra's crest, is Mt Whitney, the second highest mountain in the US – but the sequoias themselves are gargantuan enough. The road that circuits the southwestern corner is open year-round; the other only in summer. If you choose to drive, take the Generals Highway, a 46-mile (74km) paved link between both parks, which passes the greatest examples of sequoias, all named for generals. The General Grant Tree, for example, is the second largest known living tree on earth at 267ft (81m) high and 107ft (33m) in circumference. But look also for the General Sherman Tree (272ft high (82m), 106ft (32m) round), the Robert E Lee Tree and the Hart Tree.

If you are hiking, take the Congress Trail Loop, which winds through several sequoia stands for 2 miles (3km), providing access to fishing areas, scenic outlooks and meadows. Seeing the parks this way, on foot – or by mule – is even more recommended than using wheels. Lodgepole Visitor Center is the starting point for guided hikes and backpack excursions, though there are other information centres at Grant and Cedar Groves.

Some of the better-known park attractions are Tunnel Log, where one of the fallen trees has created what looks like a doorway, Beadle Rock, a vantage point at sunset, and Moro Rock, from where you can see the Great Western Divide mountain range. Strange geographical formations are found in Crystal Cave – a park ranger will explain them. Relics on Hospital Rock relate to the Mono Indians, once the area's inhabitants. Another interesting sight is Tharp's Log, a log cabin in a hollow sequoia. It was used by explorer Hale Tharp.

Some say the greatest natural beauty is at Mineral King where there are sub-alpine meadows. The area may be reached 25 miles (40km) south of Three Rivers in Sequoia National Park. The least explored sections of Kings Canyon lie in the centre where lake and mountain beauty awaits hikers.

Campsites are scattered throughout both parks and there are stores and supply centres for obtaining provisions and fishing licences. Mules and horses may be rented at Giant Forest, Grant Grove, Cedar Grove, Mineral King and Owens Valley.

♦

SHASTA LAKE

This, the state's largest man-made lake, is a recreational area formed by the Shasta Dam which backs up the Sacramento, McCloud and Pit Rivers in northern California. With 370 miles (595km) of shoreline and a surface area of 30,000 acres, its watersport potential is one of the best. A few days on a houseboat, for instance, is one of the more unusual ways to enjoy the region. Other types of boat are available for rent and may indeed be necessary to reach some of the campsites maintained by the Forest Service.

Certainly the only way to reach Shasta Caverns is by boat. A ferry service operates year-round (2 miles (3km) off Interstate 5) to take visitors across the lake. Tour buses on the other side are the transport for the short scenic trip up 800ft (240m) of mountainside to the caverns. They comprise a series of large connected caves where miniature waterfalls and countless stalactites and stalagmites have become a visual fairy-tale wonderland.

◆
SOLVANG

Does this sound like a Danish name? It is, for Solvang (meaning 'Sunny Valley') was founded by Danish settlers in 1911. This small town in Santa Ynez Valley north of Santa Barbara is pleasantly rural, its buildings and windmills featuring 'bingingsvaerk' walls, typical of Danish hamlets in the Middle Ages. Many of the shops here sell Danish goods and its cafés serve Scandinavian cuisine; tribute to northern roots is paid each September when a special festival brings out all those with Danish national costume.

The General Sherman Tree in Sequoia National Park

Two Solvang musts are a ride on a horse-drawn street car and a visit to St Ines Mission on the eastern outskirts of town. The peaceful Santa Ynez Valley serves as a city escape hatch. It is studded with horse farms and scenic parks of which the most popular is **Nojoqui Falls Park**, named for the 164ft (50m) falls.

◆
VENTURA

Both a mission town and seaside resort, Ventura is a good vacation base 70 miles (112km) northwest from Los Angeles. Mission San Buenaventura is in the centre of town – it's the ninth in the chain and the last to be founded by Father Serra. It is especially noted for lovely gardens and an archaeological museum.

Sandy beaches, surfing and fishing areas give Ventura its sporting outlook. A scheduled boat service operates to the offshore Channel Islands National Park, and, 15 miles (24km) inland, the Ojai Valley offers cultural events and other activities.

♦♦♦
YOSEMITE

Being the grandest and most splendid of California's national parks, Yosemite is a holiday area in its own right. Thanks to conservation campaigner, John Muir, it became the state's first park by Act of Congress in 1864. The focal point for the majority of holiday-makers is the 7 miles (11km) of meadow and forest that make up Yosemite Valley, where there are campsites and other lodgings and facilities. This is where you can shop for food, and it is also possible to rent a horse. A summer sightseeing tour of Yosemite takes in the highest waterfall, Yosemite Falls. In summer one can take the winding road to panoramic Glacier Point or hike the Four Mile Trail, a steep, zig-zag descent to the valley floor. There are hiking trails in the park to suit both the novice and the expert, and short horse or mule trips can easily be arranged. However, trips to the back country do need a special permit (available from the ranger stations) and fishing the park's streams and rivers requires a licence. Gateway to the high country is Tuolumne, an alpine meadow with its own summer campsite and naturalist programmes.

In winter most roads are closed, but the main valley activity centre continues to operate during the winter months, and has its own outdoor skating rink. Wintersport enthusiasts will find plenty of trails for cross-country skiing as well as downhill runs at Badger Pass. Ski equipment can be rented during the season which runs from around mid-December to early April.

Yosemite National Park, in the heart of the Sierra Nevada

PEACE AND QUIET

Wildlife and Countryside in California

California is a strikingly beautiful state with one of the most varied terrains in the whole of North America. Although famous for its coastline, you can leave the Pacific, cross immense valleys to reach snow-capped mountains and finish up in barren deserts, all in a day! The marine life around the coast is rich and varied. Since the prevailing winds are from the west, the coastal lowlands have a mild climate with plenty of rainfall. However, in southern California in particular, mountain ranges relieve the winds of most of their moisture, so the plains beyond them have become the parched Mojave and Colorado deserts.

California's wildlife is as rich and varied as its terrain. Blue whales, the largest living animals, are sometimes seen offshore, and the largest living things the world has ever known, the giant sequoias, still persist in the Sierra Nevada. Over 400 species of bird have been recorded in the state.

The Coastline

Much of California's coast is rugged, beautiful and varied. The northern half of the Californian coast is influenced by the cold Japanese current which sweeps down from Alaska as far as Point Conception, north of Los Angeles. Further south, the coastline swings sharply eastward, leaving the cold waters to swing away from the shore and warmer waters push up from the south.

The north/south divide influences the wildlife as well as the climate. In the north, the coastal redwood thrives, particularly at Muir Woods to the north of San Francisco Bay. Though smaller than their giant relative, these trees are still impressive and inspiring. The coastline is dramatic and never more so than at Point Reyes National Seashore, an easy drive north from San Francisco. Here, northern sea-lions bark in the surf and shorebirds such as black oystercatcher, black turnstone and willet feed on the beaches.

In southern California, the most conspicuous birds of the shoreline are the gulls. Ring-billed, Western and Californian gulls are common and will often come to food. In all months of the year except June, they are joined by the elegant Heerman's gull, a visitor from Mexico, and winter months bring northern visitors such as glaucous-winged gulls. Shorebirds and pelicans are common along the southern coast, and piers and jetties are often visited by Californian sea-lions, the familiar 'performing seal' of circuses. Keep a careful eye on the sea itself and you may be lucky enough to spot a spouting gray whale. They often migrate close inshore, moving south in December and January and north again in March and April, to and from their calving grounds in Baja California.

Marshes and Wetlands

Wetland areas occur throughout California from the coastal lagoons which attract waders at high tide, to the desert oases miles inland. The bottom of Central Valley, west of Enterprise, was at one time the winter haunt for tens of millions of wetland birds and, although drainage and agriculture have altered this forever, there are still areas protected from change. The Gray Lodge Waterfowl Area in Central Valley, for example, still attracts over a million ducks and geese in winter. The commonest ducks are pintail, American wigeon, lesser scaup and ruddy duck, but they can be joined by up to 15 other species, depending on the size and location of the water. Long-billed curlews haunt the marshy margins alongside American coots. This concentration of wildlife inevitably attracts a variety of predators such as red-tailed and the more unusual Swainson's hawks.

Wherever it is found, water acts like a magnet to the wildlife of the surrounding countryside and this influence is most profound in dry sagebrush and desert regions where mammals and birds come to drink and bathe. However, wetland areas not only attract the resident wildlife but serve as stopping-off points for birds on migration. Birdwatchers have long known this and a day's outing is not complete without a visit to a marsh.

To get the best out of wetland birdwatching, it is useful to know a few 'tricks of the trade'. Ducks and waders are

Long-billed curlews often call loudly in flight

normally easy to see, but many of the smaller birds prefer to skulk in the bushes, their calls being the only thing which gives their presence away. The way to draw these secretive birds out into the open is to 'pish'. This technique, which only seems to work with American birds, involves making a series of abrupt hissing sounds through clenched teeth. A burst of short, high-pitched squeaks sometimes has a similar effect, and the National Audubon Society sells ready-made wooden squeakers for this very purpose. Try it anywhere and you will be amazed what pops out of the bushes!

Southern Mountains

Although they lack the grandeur of the Sierra Nevada further north, southern California can boast two major mountain ranges of its own. The Transverse Range runs east from Point Conception and holds the Santa Monica, San Gabriel and San Bernardino mountains, while the Peninsular Range, which runs south into Baja California, comprises the Santa Ana, Palomar and Laguna mountains.

The summit of Mount Pinos, nearly 9,000ft (2,700m) above sea-level, is as good a place as any to see the wildlife of the southern mountains. A road leads to a car park near the summit and from here the visitor can explore the surrounding area. Californian ground squirrels and grey squirrels are common and

often oblivious to people. If you make the return trip down the mountain at dusk you stand a good chance of seeing some of the more unusual mammals. Bobcats, coyotes and mule deer all haunt the woodland and if you are really lucky you may see a black bear. Bears may look cuddly and friendly, but they are often unpredictable. If you do see one it is best to watch it from the safety of your car.

The largest bird likely to be seen is the golden eagle and patient observers often get very good views as the birds soar overhead.

In the trees is a wealth of birdlife from woodpeckers to owls, while calliope humming-birds frequent the glades. The Clark's nutcracker noisily eats seeds from pine cones and its white face is conspicuous even at a distance.

Deserts

Lying in the rainshadow of the southern mountains are California's eastern deserts – barren lands where rainfall is infrequent and erratic. Despite drought and heat, deserts hold a fascinating variety of specialised plants and animals and have a unique charm. Although they grade into one another, the two major deserts are very different in character. To the north of the region, the Mojave desert occupies land 1–4,000ft (300–1,000m) above sea-level, whereas to the south the Colorado desert stretches from Salton to the Mexican border and lies at lower altitudes. Some areas of the

PEACE AND QUIET

Joshua trees are a characteristic feature of the Mojave desert

desert are actually below sea-level, culminating in the fearful Death Valley which, at minus 282ft (86m), is the lowest point in North America.

The Joshua Tree National Monument, which lies across the San Andreas Fault, contains 872 square miles (2,258sq km) of both Mojave and Colorado desert. The name 'Joshua tree' was coined by westward-trekking Mormons who thought they resembled Joshua at prayer. These imposing plants, which are a species of yucca and only occur here above an altitude of about 3,000ft (900m), are crucial to the survival of much desert life. They provide nesting sites for 25 species of birds, shade from the noon-day sun for mammals and lizards, and their flowers provide

nectar for yucca moths. Despite the lack of water, the deserts harbour many well-adapted mammals. Nocturnal species avoid the sun's rays, but pronghorn antelope and desert bighorn sheep seem indifferent to the heat. A night drive through the desert may reveal coyotes and desert kangaroo rats caught in the car's headlights. Kangaroo rats are endearing creatures which are seemingly fearless of man. Deserts are much favoured by reptiles. The desert iguana haunts the vicinity of creosote bushes in the low desert, and the chuckwalla, California's largest lizard, occurs around rocky outcrops. However, the desert's most renowned inhabitants are the rattlesnakes, of which several species can be found. The

Western diamond-backed rattlesnake is particularly common and is sometimes seen crossing roads.

Salton Sea

Despite the fact that this lake is effectively man-made, it is frequented by vast numbers of birds: half a million ducks alone spend the winter here and the flocks comprise up to 20 species. The margins of the lake and the surrounding land support up to 50,000 wintering geese including Canada, snow and the rare Ross' goose. Almost any shorebird present on the coast is likely to turn up on the Salton Sea and up to six species of heron and egret are regularly seen. A careful search of the flocks of birds may even reveal the unusual white-faced ibis, a speciality of the area. Dead trees around the edge of the lake provide ideal perches for America's national emblem, the bald eagle, conspicuous with its white head and white tail, and, from July to September, the Salton Sea also attracts unusual birds from Mexico such as wood stork, blue-footed and brown boobies and black skimmers.

The rough 'brush' country surrounding the lake contains typical dry-habitat animals. Cactus wrens adorn elevated perches, and burrowing owls and roadrunners are common ground dwellers, the latter feeding on lizards which abound in the area. Snakes are also common here and include the venomous sidewinder rattlesnake.

Yosemite National Park

Yosemite is California's most famous National Park and contains well over 1,000 square miles (2,500sq km) of awe-inspiring scenery set in the High Sierras. Immense trees complement the grand scale of the glaciated rock formations which tower above the central Yosemite Valley, itself already 4,000ft (1,200m) above sea-level.

Initial access to the park is through Yosemite Valley, which is dominated by two dramatic rock formations so beloved of rock climbers. El Capitan has a sheer rock-face 3,500ft (1,066m) high, and the famous Half Dome rises 4,800ft (1,460m) above the Tenaya Valley below. Almost everything about Yosemite is majestic, including the 620ft-high (188m) Bridalveil falls. Yosemite is geared up for visitors. In the summer months the valley floor can be packed with people but, as is the case with most American parks, the number of tourists drops off dramatically after Labor Day. Even if the park is crowded when you visit, you can easily escape the hordes by following one of the numerous tracks or route-marked trails. It is amazing how few people stray further than a few hundred yards from information centres and car parks. From the valley you can easily reach the aptly named Mirror Lake, in which flowering dogwoods cast beautiful reflections. The Tuolumne Meadows, at 8,600ft (2,600m) high, are red with

PEACE AND QUIET

the flowers of the Indian paintbrush plant.

Sequoia National Park

High in the Sierra Nevada lies the Sequoia National Park, 604 square miles (1,564sq km) of land containing the deepest canyons in the state and the world's largest living trees. As a result of thoughtful planning, many hundreds of miles of trails have been laid out for hikers, and some of North America's highest mountains can be seen from ridges in the park. For the first-time visitor, the scale of the scenery and trees will take the breath away.

Giant sequoias, *Sequoiadendron giganteum*, were once widespread across North America. However, the Ice Age wiped out most of their kind and they are now restricted to high altitudes in the Sierra Nevada. Sequoia and nearby Kings Canyon National Parks are the two most accessible places to see these giants.

Giant sequoias (also confusingly known as redwoods but a different species to the tall coastal redwoods) are not only the largest living things in the world but are also among the oldest. Many individuals are thought to be over 2,000 years old and are second only, in terms of age, to the bristlecone pine, a relict population of which is found in the nearby White Mountain range.

As in Yosemite National Park, mule deer, squirrels, chipmunks and black bear are frequently seen or heard. Black bears can be troublesome and noisy nocturnal visitors to campsites; campers are advised not to keep food in their tents! Sadly, it was in this park that the last wild grizzly bear in California was seen: all the others had been hunted to extinction and this female was thought to have died after a solitary old age. The height of the trees makes birdwatching somewhat uncomfortable, but the reward of seeing a white-headed woodpecker or a great grey owl should make up for this.

Mono Lake

A visit to Mono Lake, set in the sagebrush of the Great Basin of California, and with its extraordinary moon-like landscape, is a unique experience. The waters of the lake support a wealth of specialised wildlife which contrasts markedly with the animals and plants of the surrounding desert.

The bizarre pinnacles and platforms which line the margins of Mono Lake are composed of a substance called tufa. These formations are similar in appearance and structure to stalagmites, being composed of the same chemical, calcium carbonate. The lake is the site of considerable environmental controversy. The waters of the Leevining River which once fed it have now been diverted to quench the thirst of the city of Los Angeles and, not surprisingly, this has caused a distinct drop in the water level

Strange pillars made of tufa line the margins of Mono Lake

of the lake. This is not only exposing more and more tufa to the erosion of wind and rain, but it is also threatening the very existence of several species of nesting birds. A quarter of California's breeding population of California gull breed on Negit Island and the black-necked grebes are also at risk. The high salinity of the water

PEACE AND QUIET

Bristlecone pines are thought to be the oldest living things

necked (northern) phalaropes in the late summer. These latter species are highly adapted waders who spend most of their lives swimming on water, picking animals off the surface.

The Oldest Living Things

High in the White Mountains of California grow the bristlecone pines, some of the oldest living things on the planet. It is extraordinary to think that many of these trees were already mature before the birth of Christ. With gnarled and twisted trunks and branches, many of the ancient bristlecone pines are thought to be over 3,000 years old, and at least one is considered to be approaching its 4,000th birthday – an awe-inspiring contrast to the modern US! The Shulman Grove, just beyond the Westguard Pass, is an easily accessible point to see the trees and, as you might expect, at nearly 10,000ft (3,000m) above sea-level, the scenery and views around the pines are spectacular. Birds of prey soar on thermals, mountain chickadees and pygmy nuthatches feed in the trees, and calliope hummingbirds somehow manage to survive up here. Lying in the rainshadow of the Sierra Nevada, there is much less rainfall in the White Mountains than in the Sierras to the west. As a result, the air is dry and clear and you can see for miles. So, even if your interest in trees is passing, the trip is worth it for the breathtaking views.

discourages all but the most specialised of freshwater creatures. However, what they lack in diversity the animals make up for in numbers, and brine flies and brine shrimps are excessively abundant. These in turn attract specialist birds such as the American avocet, and vast numbers of migratory Wilson's and red-

FOOD AND DRINK

California spells fruit – and more fruit. Where groves of orange trees once stood is now the site of Disneyland, but there are still countless orchards for citrus fruits, peaches, avocados, dates and walnuts. They grow mostly in the south where the weather is good year-round. Fruits may be bought freshly at farmers' markets.

California also spells seafood – and more seafood. Fat shrimp, crab, abalone, swordfish, fresh tuna, red snapper – these and other delicacies are on the menus of California's restaurants. One of the best places to go for lunch is San Francisco's waterfront where seafood may be bought by the carton.

Mexico has exerted a strong influence on Californian cuisine. *Guacamole* and *tomales* are not only generally available but are also authentic in every part of the state, most especially in San Diego.

Of all the other ethnic groups who have brought their culinary talents to Californian kitchens, the Orientals have probably had most influence. The original Trader Vic's opened in San Francisco and no one should miss eating out at one of this city's Chinatown restaurants.

Steaks and prime rib are still an important part of any menu out West – going back to the days when enormous cattle ranches gave California its most important industry. Salad to accompany the meal is always welcome, and Californian salads are excellent (try the famous Green Goddess dressing which was invented in San Francisco). Other local specialities include *cioppino*, a soup cum stew made from seafood, and San Francisco's sourdough bread. Martini, too, is associated with the area (it is said to have first been concocted in San Francisco). But perhaps the area's best-known speciality is its wine. The Napa and Sonoma Valleys, north of San Francisco, are the most famous for wine and it is easy for tourists with a hired car to travel along the 'wine roads'. One of the earliest vineyards of note was Buena Vista in Sonoma County, founded by a Hungarian. Nowadays, there are many more vineyards to visit in the Sonoma Valley, including Sebastiani and Glen Ellen. Most of them offer tours and tastings, as indeed do those wineries located in the Napa Valley. Here, you'll find Inglenook, Charles Krug and Rutherford Hill. Not content with the familiar tried and tested, California's innovative and promotional streak brought both the 'blush' wine (a very pale *rosé* made with zinfandel grapes) and the wine cooler (a light wine and fruit mixture) to widespread attention.

Finally, like anywhere else in the US, this state has numerous fast food outlets – anything from fish and chips to hamburgers and *tacos* – for quick and inexpensive options.

SHOPPING

Of course you can find anything and everything to buy in California, whether you choose to browse in major department stores, boutiques, shopping malls or main street shops in smaller towns.

The following are among the most not-to-be-missed and established:

Bazaar del Mundo is in the Old Town district of San Diego where boutiques and craft shops are now located. Note the strong Spanish/Mexican influences on goods in this 'birthplace of California'. While in San Diego, shop at Squibob Square and on the outskirts of the quarter.

The Cannery is a multi-level shopping complex that covers half a block of San Francisco's waterfront. It was converted from a fruit and vegetable canning plant in the 1960s. Nowadays, chic boutiques and eating places surround a pleasant central courtyard.

Chinatown in San Francisco brims with things Oriental. Its major thoroughfare is Grant Avenue.

Embarcadero Center is the name given to the 8½ acres of shopping malls between San Francisco's financial district and waterfront. Around noon you'll find many stalls selling leather items and jewellery.

El Paseo in Palm Desert, one of the satellite communities of Palm Springs, is known as the Rodeo Drive of the desert because of its high-priced boutiques. It is a beautiful 2-mile-long (3km) street lined with exclusive stores and art galleries. It is well worth looking at but shopping here will make a dent in the wallet.

Fisherman's Village at Marina del Rey, on the edge of Los Angeles, has been designed to simulate a New England fishing village. It is a good place to look for small gift items. Not far away, at the Venice edge of Marina del Rey, is Port of Craft, where a cluster of shops specialise in arts and crafts.

Ghirardelli Square, like The Cannery, is a converted San Francisco waterfront complex (it used to be a chocolate factory). The goods sold from its multi-levels come from all over the world.

Lido Village at Newport Beach, south of Los Angeles, boasts rows of smart shops which open onto brick walkways or front onto the wharf. Also visit Cannery Village, which stretches for five blocks along the wharf and includes artists' stalls.

Olvera Street, at the heart of downtown Los Angeles, is a block-long, pedestrianised Mexican market-place with shops and cafés.

Pier 39, on the waterfront of San Francisco, is a bustling shopping complex, rebuilt with the wood from other demolished piers.

Ports O'Call and Whaler's Wharf, in San Pedro (LA), offer a combination of Mediterranean seaport atmosphere and colonial-style stores and taverns.

Rodeo Drive, at the core of Beverly Hills, is patronised by the rich and famous. Its elegant shops sell prestigious labels at very high prices.

Shopping in America has always been an experience, either in covered multi-storey complexes which are filled with greenery and specially designed to be light and airy, or in clever conversions or 'themed' complexes, perhaps with a nautical or colonial emphasis. The latter are, of course, where you'll find unique boutiques and gift shops, art galleries and collectable items.

Something else the US has generally got right is its museum shops. Though some of the items may well be 'kitsch', you'll probably be surprised at some of the unusual pieces that are displayed, and, naturally, that goes for prints and posters as well. Theme parks, too, all sell gifts, some the fairground kind, but some, such as Disneyland's soft toys, are excellent buys as presents.

Large department stores also have their charm especially if you have time to sift through the array of goods. Frequent sales and discount offers can result in a bargain if you're careful and choosey. American-made clothing is generally available in a wide range of sizes and colours, and American designer labels are obviously cheaper than when purchased in other parts of the world. Don't skip the sportswear shops at golf and tennis resorts either – their T-shirts and track suits are often excellent.

ACCOMMODATION

The range of accommodation in California is as good as, if not better than, in any other state. There are many prestigious properties but there are just as many chain hotels/motels in the popular areas and along the highways. Names to look for that always offer good value for money include Quality Inn, Howard Johnson, Holiday Inn, TraveLodge and Vagabond. Visitors will find resort hotels with every facility on site in holiday areas like the Desert Communities close to Palm Springs. They will also find rustic lodge accommodation (as well as campsites) in parks such as Yosemite, and they will find cosy small inns at destinations like Carmel and around the wine valleys of Napa and Sonoma.

Holiday apartments are available for those interested in self-catering – the greatest choice is in the beach areas. And for those who enjoy the idea of bed and breakfast, there are plenty of delightful privately owned guest houses.

NIGHTLIFE

There is no lack of nightlife in the big cities, where anything goes from strip joints to symphony orchestras. The best way to find out what's currently on where is (a) to ask at your hotel, (b) to look at any visitor publications that might be in your hotel room or (c) to obtain details from the city visitors' and convention bureau. In San Francisco this is at 1390

WEATHER

Market St, tel: (415) 626 5500, in Los Angeles at 505 S Flower, tel: (213) 488 9100, and in San Diego at 1200 3rd Ave, tel: (619) 232 3101.

WEATHER AND WHEN TO GO

California has its share of sun, and usually accepts casual dress everywhere, though top hotels and restaurants may require jackets and ties for dining and may have rules about no bare feet or beachwear in their lobby. But the state's climate is extremely variable and how you dress may well depend on your destination. San Francisco, for example, can be cool and rainy, whilst Los Angeles and southern California may be hot and sticky. Desert areas can have summer temperatures of well over 40 degrees C (100 degrees F); mountain areas on the other hand can get really chilly. If you plan to tour, 'layered clothing' is ideal, and comfortable shoes for sightseeing are an essential. Oddly enough, the Americans are more prudish than you might expect so women should check first before going topless on a beach or by a pool – it may be frowned upon. Nude sunbathing is not on unless stipulated otherwise.

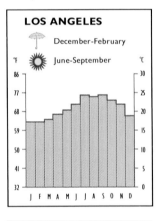

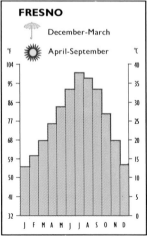

FESTIVALS AND EVENTS

January
Desert Communities – celebrity golf tournaments
Pasadena (LA) – Tournament of Roses Parade and games
South Lake Tahoe – winter carnival

February
Indio (Desert Communities) – National Date Festival
Los Angeles and San Francisco – impressive Chinese New Year celebrations
Monterey – Film Festival

March
Long Beach (LA) – Congressional Cup Sailing Race
Monterey – wine festival
Rancho Mirage (Desert Communities) – ladies' golfing tournament
Sacramento – Camellia Festival
San Juan Capistrano – Heritage 'Return of the Swallows' Festival
Santa Barbara – international orchid show
Santa Cruz – jazz festival

April
Bakersfield – Heritage Days with parade and ethnic food
Long Beach (LA) – Grand Prix
Monterey – adobe tour
Red Bluff – rodeo and parade
Redding – Dixieland Jazz Festival
Santa Barbara – 2-week-long Arts Festival

May
Central Valley – Shasta Damboree
Healdsburg – Russian River Winefest including food and crafts
Petaluma – Living History days to celebrate the 1840s
Sacramento – Dixieland Jazz Jubilee
San Jose – Cinco de Mayo celebrations
San Luis Obispo – La Fiesta with food, music and entertainment

June
Del Mar (near San Diego) – county fair
Mammoth Lakes – motocross at its best, on one of the finest tracks
Red Bluff – Arts Festival
St Helena – Napa Valley wine auction
Santa Barbara – summer sports festival
Sonoma – ox roast
Tuolumne (Yosemite) – Lumber Jubilee with parade and games

July
San José – arts festival
Santa Cruz – Cabrillo Music Festival
NB Many areas celebrate 4 July in a variety of ways. There are also summer festivals throughout the state.

August
Clear Lake – Blackberry Festival
Sacramento – State Fair
Sonoma – county wine showcase and auction

September
San Diego – Cabrillo Festival
Solvang – Danish Days
Sonoma – Vintage Festival with tastings and re-enactment of 'Bear Flag Revolt'

October
San Francisco – Grand National Livestock Exposition, rodeo and horse show

November
Hollywood (LA) – Christmas parade

December – many Christmas celebrations throughout State

CHILDREN

One thing is for sure, youngsters will have plenty to keep them amused in California, over and above adventure sports and the beach. If they are too young to appreciate culture, they won't be too young for the plethora of waxwork museums, laser shows, sea-aquariums and theme parks.
San Diego's zoo is one of the best in the country, but other wildlife and safari parks are dotted throughout the state. American theme parks are, without doubt, the best designed in the world. Disneyland is tops, of course, but there are others like Magic Mountain, Great America and Knott's Berry Farm.
Few chain motels charge for under 12's sharing a room; coffee shops and fast food outlets often list a children's menu.

HOW TO BE A LOCAL

'Laid-back' is the key phrase for life in California. This is the easy-going State, where there is generally no such thing as formality. San Francisco particularly, with its great variety of communities and traditions, has an open, cosmopolitan atmosphere. If you relax and have a good time you will already be halfway to behaving like a local.

TIGHT BUDGET

Self-catering is an excellent way to keep family costs down – American supermarkets are large and well stocked. Alternatively, look for motel accommodation that allows up to four to share the same room for one price. (Children's age limit varies from 12 to 18.) Such motels are clean, comfortable, feature two double beds and usually offer a free coffee/tea-making facility.
Look for restaurants offering all-you-can-eat meals for a fixed price, help-yourself salad bars and children's menus. Many of these are situated along the highways. Save money on drinks at 'Happy Hour' time when two-for-the-price-of-one are on offer.
Don't bother with an organised city tour of San Francisco either – it's easy enough to get around by bus, tram or on foot. Do, on the other hand, take tours of Los Angeles as it is difficult to get around without a car.
Make the most of the free entertainment, both in theme parks and on the street, like Fisherman's Wharf, San Francisco.
Similarly, pick vineyards which offer free tours and tastings and visit museums and galleries which are free – local newspapers and tourist publications will give listings.

DIRECTORY

Arriving

International direct flights operate to Los Angeles, one of the world's busiest airports. It is the major air terminal for southern California. However, many international charter flights use San Diego airport. International flights to the north of the state arrive at one of the three airports in the San Francisco Bay area. San Francisco is the major handler, but Oakland deals with many international charter flights, as does San José. Major American airlines operating international flights to/from these airports include American, Delta, Northwest, Pan Am and TWA. Many of these offer a fly/drive programme (see **Driving**).

It is easy enough to fly between cities on shuttle or feeder service flights, but these short hops can be expensive. Anyone planning short-leg flights, or adding California to another American destination, may be better off investing in a Visit USA pass. US Air offer a West Coast USA pass for travel between Los Angeles, San Francisco, Las Vegas and San Diego; the cost is $109 (for $129 you can travel within California, as well as Arizona, Nevada and New Mexico).

Travel Documents Visas are required by all visitors to the US, except for Canadian citizens, or British citizens visiting the US for business or tourist purposes, for a stay not exceeding 90 days, and provided that a return ticket is being held. In these instances a passport only is required. However, rules at city gateways vary about transit stops and visitors may not be able to re-enter the US (after a quick visit to Canada or Mexico, for example) without a visa. It is best to double check the requirements for any specific holiday plans before departure. The type and validity of US visas vary considerably and detailed information should be sought from the nearest US Embassy or Consulate. Suffice to say that the Americans are quite strict in these matters and passengers whose travel documents are not in order will not be accepted for travel in the US under any circumstances.

Camping

All the natural scenic areas boast well run camp sites which include facilities for those who don't like to 'rough it' too much. Especially recommended are those in the national parks such as Lassen Volcanic Park, Redwood, Sequoia and King's Canyon, Anza-Borrego Desert State Park, Death Valley and Yosemite. Some parks impose camping limits of 7 to 15 days in summer (winter in desert areas). For some beach parks and parks near major urban areas reservations are required in summer and at weekends. Further information on state park campsites (including reservations up to eight weeks in advance) can

DIRECTORY

be obtained by writing to: Reservations, Department of Parks and Recreation, Box 942896, Sacramento, CA 94296-0420.

Car Hire
See **Domestic Travel**, Driving

Chauffeur Driven Cars
Easy to arrange, but expensive. Some hotels, especially the higher class ones, provide a complimentary limousine service to and from airports. From the international airports there is a 'public' limousine service – these perform a shuttle service from airport to hotel at less than the cost of a taxi. These airport limousines are not to be confused with the luxurious, sedan-type, private limousine. Bookings for chauffeur drive for US destinations may be made before you leave home through certain international car rental companies.

Crime
California is certainly not crime free and drugs are a problem, but exercise due caution in the major cities, especially in the downtown areas, and you should be safe. In an emergency dial 911 and ask for police, fire or ambulance.

Customs Regulations
Non-US residents may bring in up to one litre of alcoholic beverages, 200 cigarettes (or 100 cigars or 3lbs (1.4kg) of tobacco) plus up to $100 worth of gifts – duty free. There is no limit to the amount of currency (US or foreign) brought into America but arriving or departing passengers must report to US Customs all money in excess of $10,000. Not allowed: drugs (other than prescribed), fresh meat, fruit, plants.

Cycling
With its 'near perfect' climate, California is a cyclist's paradise. In the city, and through the natural beauty of the state, cycle paths are in evidence, most of them well laid-out. Two popular routes are Sunset Bikeway on the outskirts of San Francisco, and the larger scale Pacific Coast Bikecentennial Route, covering the entire central coast area. It is easy to hire a bicycle, bicycle rental agencies abound (look in Yellow Pages), and most of the public transport systems accommodate passengers with bikes.

Domestic Travel
Driving You need only a valid driving licence from your country to rent a car in California, though an International Driver's Permit is sometimes required of visitors from certain countries. Most car rental companies require the driver to be at least 21, though some companies will rent to drivers of only 18. Touring California by car is certainly one of the best ways of seeing this varied state. Major roads are well-surfaced, wide and well signposted. Local roads are not so well surfaced and are often narrow. The American terminology is freeways, or interstate roads, for motorways, while other

roads are collectively known as highways. Toll roads also exist; they are known as superhighways and charge 2-3 cents per mile, but with petrol at only about $1 per gallon (4.5 litres) they are affordable. The national speed limit is 55/65 miles (88/105km) per hour. On city highways and in congested areas it is generally between 25-35 miles (40-56km) per hour. Road signs indicate specific limits which are strictly enforced - so are *minimum* speed limits on city freeways. And a word of warning about driving in Los Angeles – it has the world's most extensive road system, so plan your route AHEAD and avoid the rush hour.

If you are planning on renting a car, consider before you go the fly/drive programmes that many airlines offer; it might well save you some money. Sometimes a car is even included in the holiday package. Otherwise most of the major car rental companies have offices throughout the state – if a rental company has an office in your own country you can arrange to pick up a car from a US destination before you depart. Charges vary depending upon size of car,but basic charges range from $25 to $50 per day, if renting in California.

Bus Greyhound Lines operates an inter-city service within California. Anyone considering using this mode of transport should think about purchasing an Ameripass (only available outside the US, passes are for 7 days, 15 days, or 30 days – prices are in the local currency of the country in which the Ameripass is purchased). Unlimited daily extensions to these periods are available at the time of purchase. These passes enable visitors to travel anywhere over Greyhound's entire route system.

Within the state, local communities and the major cities are served by local bus services. San Francisco in addition has cable cars (national historic landmarks), operating across the downtown area – the flat fare is $2. San Diego has a trolley car service through the downtown area to the border with Mexico.

Taxi Taxis may be hailed on the street but few cruise outside areas of heavy tourist concentration in California, so if you are away from airports or major hotels it is best to phone for one (look under 'cabs' in Yellow Pages). When you do manage to find one, fares are likely to be from about $1.20 to $3 for the first mile, and $1.60 to $1.80 for each additional mile.

Rail Inter-city rail service is provided by America's National Railroad Corporation – Amtrak. A special Far Western Region Rail Pass is available for purchase outside the US – at time of printing, $159 for 45 days of unlimited travel over the far western states, $79.50 for children.

Electricity
The standard electricity supply in the US is 110 volts (60 cycles), in comparison with the

DIRECTORY

more powerful 220 volts (50 cycles) of most of Europe, Africa and parts of the Far East. Electrical appliances from the latter areas (or any using 220 volts) not fitted with dual-voltage capability will require a voltage transformer to render them safe for use. To avoid accidents these are best purchased before leaving home, though converter kits are available from electrical stores in the US. Also, electrical connections may be different from those you are used to at home. US sockets accept plugs with two flat pins in a parallel position, with in addition an upper, round, earth pin for earthed appliances such as an iron. Outside the US, Canada, South America, the Caribbean and Japan an electrical adaptor (different from a voltage transformer) will be required to run appliances brought from home (once it has been established they are safe for 110 volts power) – they too can be purchased before leaving home.

Health

It cannot be emphasised enough that arranging medical insurance before travelling is essential. Medical facilities are generally of an extremely high standard in California, as they are in the rest of the US, but costs are exorbitant. Insurance cover for an unlimited amount of medical costs is to be recommended. Service will be refused without evidence of some kind of insurance, or a deposit if no insurance. If you need a doctor during your stay, ask at your hotel or look in the Yellow Pages under 'Physician' (see also **Pharmacist**, for less serious cases).
No inoculations are required for a visit to California.

Holidays

New Year's Day (Jan 1), Martin Luther King, Jr's Birthday (third Mon in Jan), Lincoln's Birthday (Feb 12), Washington's Birthday (third Mon in Feb), Memorial Day (last Mon in May), Independence Day (July 4), Labor day (first Mon in Sept), Admission Day (Sept 9), Columbus Day (second Mon in Oct), Veterans' Day (Nov 11), Thanksgiving (4th Thurs in Nov), Christmas Day (Dec 25).

Money Matters

As a general rule, banks are open from 09.00 to 15.00 Mon–Fri and are closed on weekends and public holidays although in some major towns and tourist areas hours may be longer. Currency may be changed at airports while some hotels feature currency exchange facilities, but it is best to go prepared with US dollar travellers' cheques (travellers' checks, in the US). The advantage of this is that US dollar travellers' cheques can be used very much like cash. Hotels, restaurants, petrol stations and shops in California will accept them as cash and give change where necessary (a useful way of topping up your cash supply without going to the bank). For this reason it is advisable to take out travellers' cheques in denominations of $10 or $20. The American monetary unit is of course the dollar, which is divided into 100 cents. The usual coins are the one cent (or penny), the five cent (nickel), the 10 cent (dime) and the 25 cent (quarter). There are also half-dollar and one-dollar coins which may appear in your change at times. Try and keep some small change ready at all times as some public transportation and telephones may require exact amounts. Dollar notes (bills) are issued in denominations of one, two five, 10, 20, 50 and 100. Be warned, though: all notes, whatever their value, are *exactly the same colour and size*. The easiest bills to work with are the $10 and $20 with a few singles for tipping. Remember that each American state levies a tax on certain items so the price tag you see may not be the price you pay. Additionally, counties and cities may levy their own tax but this varies.

You can of course use credit cards almost anywhere. If you run out of money, look in the Yellow Pages for foreign exchange brokers or head for American Express. There is no limit to the amount of foreign currency you bring in or take out of America (see **Customs**).

Motoring Organisation – Benefits

The two motoring organisations covering California are the California State Automobile Association (CSAA) and the Automobile Club of Southern California (ACSC). They are both affiliated clubs of the American Automobile Association (AAA) which itself is a member of the International Touring Alliance (AIT). As such, the CSAA and the ACSC make certain services available to member organisations from other countries. Check your eligibility to services while in the US with your own club. CSAA and ACSC offices are in most large towns, ports and airports and are able to offer travel related assistance upon production of a valid AIT affiliated membership certificate.

Emergency Road Service The AAA operates a nationwide emergency road service number. If you require assistance while travelling in the US, call 1-800-336-HELP. And if you are involved in a traffic accident it must be reported to the local police station.

Pharmacist

Quick remedy medicines such as aspirin are readily available at any pharmacy (drug store). Tablets containing acetaminophen correspond to tablets containing paracetamol in other countries.

Post Office

Some main post offices stay open 24 hours a day, but, as a rule, hours are 08.00 to 18.00 Monday to Friday and 08.00 to 12.00 on Saturdays. Stamps for mail abroad are available from machines in drug stores – however, you will pay over the odds for these.

DIRECTORY

Sport and Recreation

California is one of the sportiest states. Due to the equable climate, participating sports are more popular than spectator sports. Surfing, scuba and skindiving, sailing, horseback riding, fishing and in a few places, dune-buggy racing, can be enjoyed throughout the year along the southern Californian coast – further north these activities are more seasonal. 'Freshwater' recreation is also important. White-water rafting is popular, commercial raft trips operating on some rivers.

Telephones

Telephones are located in hotel lobbies, drug stores, restaurants, garages and in roadside kiosks. Exact change in 5 cent, 10 cent and 25 cent pieces is required to place a call, except in the case of an emergency when you should just dial '0' for the operator. The first minute of domestic long distance calls, and first three minutes of international calls must be paid for before your call can be placed. California does have a direct dial system – to dial abroad, dial 1, followed by the country code, followed by the city code, followed by the number.

Time

California is on Pacific Standard Time; in reverse of the time in Britain by 8 hours, Australia (Sydney) 18 hours, Japan 17 hours, Brazil (Rio de Janeiro) 5 hours.

Tipping

Tipping in restaurants is widely practised as service charges are not normally included in the bill – 15 to 20 per cent of the total bill is usually expected (more for dinner than lunch). Taxi drivers and hairdressers should be similarly tipped.

Toilets

Public toilets are almost always of a high standard. They are known as 'Rest Rooms', and are usually free.

Tourist Offices

Several offices will provide free information to visitors. The California Office of Tourism, 1121 L Street, Suite 103, Sacramento, CA 95814 (tel: 916-322-1396) will help guide you to areas throughout the state. For information on northern California contact: Redwood Empire Association, 1 Market Plaza, Suite 1001, San Francisco, CA 94105 (tel: 415-543-8334). For more specific information, ask for the local chamber of commerce and information centres.

Whale Watching

Every year from mid December to February the Californian gray whales swim southward along the northern and central Californian coasts. The return trip is made from March to mid May. Whale watching cruises are undertaken by Marine Mammal Fund, San Francisco (tel: 415-775-4636); Tides Wharf, Box 547, Bodega Bay (tel: 707-875-3595); and King Salmon Charters, 5333 Herrick Road, Eureka (tel: 707-442-3474).

INDEX